I0811501

Nurturing Spiritual Development in Children

by Understanding Our Own Spirituality

Ester R.A. Leutenberg and Deborah L. Schein, PhD
Illustrator, Amy Leutenberg Brodsky, LISW-S

WholePerson
Mental Health & Wellness
publisher of therapy, counseling, and self-help resources

101 West 2nd Street, Suite 203
Duluth, MN 55802

800-247-6789

Books@WholePerson.com
WholePerson.com

Nurturing Spiritual Development in Children
by Understanding Our Own Spirituality

Copyright ©2017 by Ester R.A. Leutenberg and Deborah L. Schein.
All rights reserved. No part of this book may be reproduced or transmitted in any form by any means, electronic or mechanical, including photocopying, without permission from the copyright holders.

All efforts have been made to ensure accuracy of the information contained in this workbook as of the date published.

The author(s) and the publisher expressly disclaim responsibility for any adverse effects arising from the use or application of the information contained herein.

Printed in the United States of America

10 9 8 7 6 5 4 3 2 1

Editorial Director: Carlene Sippola
Art Director: Mathew Pawlak

Library of Congress Control Number: 2016960385
ISBN: 978-157025-350-8

Nurturing Spiritual Development in Children by Understanding Our Own Spirituality

Introduction

The purpose of this book, *Nurturing Spiritual Development in Children by Understanding Our Own Spirituality,* is to encourage caregivers to be aware of the importance of spirituality and to realize that spiritual development can be nurtured at very young ages.

The term caregiver refers to biological, adoptive, step or foster parents; family members, child-care educators; day-care workers and nannies; and other people who are in the position of being responsible for the care of young children.

A caregiver can begin instilling spirituality even before a child is born. Singing and other sounds are felt as vibrations and possibly as sounds by a fetus in the womb. During this time frame, an infant is most vulnerable to the environment. A baby absorbs and adapts to time, place, region, and local norms and culture. The spiritual embryonic phase begins here and continues throughout one's lifetime.

This book introduces the concept of spiritual development vital for all caregivers, for it references aspects of spiritual development that are common to all people. The intent of the authors of this book is to provide opportunities to evoke and strengthen each caregiver's spiritual development, and ultimately, influence the spiritual development of the children to whom the adults are giving care.

Each chapter offers insight into how spiritual development unfolds. Within each chapter, readers will find information about various aspects of spiritual development. Space is given for reflection and journal writing. This will provide opportunities to evoke and strengthen the caregivers' spiritual development that will enhance the spiritual development of the children the adults are nurturing.

TRUE-ISMS

Young Children and Spiritual Development

- Spirituality is an innate human trait.
- This innate trait must be nurtured in order to flourish.
- All children require love and attachment at the beginning of life to awaken this innate spirituality, so that it can be nurtured and developed.
- All children need interesting and beautiful spaces in which to experience life. This space can be as big as a park, and as small as a corner of a room.
- Young children are extremely competent learners because they have absorbent minds with exceptional ability to learn culture, language, and nuances from the environment and the people in that environment.
- Spiritual development plays an important role in promoting learning and growth for all children, and is inter-related with all other domains of development.
- Children will develop spirituality far more easily when the adults in their lives are spiritually grounded.

© 2017 WHOLE PERSON ASSOCIATES, 101 WEST 2ND STREET, SUITE 203, DULUTH MN 55802 • 800-247-6789 • WHOLEPERSON.COM

Definitions of Terms Involved with Spiritual Development

Acceptance – acts of tolerance, openness, and empathy towards cultures different from one's own.

Awe – a feeling of respect or reverence. Awe is often inspired by something majestic, powerful, unbelievable, or even scary. Awe is also stimulated by spiritual moments that connect to and strengthen one's basic dispositions.

Basic disposition – internal feeling triggered by moments of wonderment, awe, joy, or inner peace.

Caregiver – biological, adoptive, step, or foster parents; family members; child-care educators, day-care workers, and nannies; and all other people who are in the position of being responsible for the care of young children.

Complex disposition – reflected in how one acts toward others by caring, kindness, empathy, and reverence.

Disposition – includes basic and complex dispositions referenced above.

Gratitude – an emotion and an attitude that emerges when one experiences positive moments and is happy and grateful about them.

Joy – a feeling of deep happiness and contentment capable of lighting up one's face. Joy is also stimulated by spiritual moments that connect to and strengthen one's basic dispositions.

Meditation – a process by which one encourages and develops a deeper ability to concentrate and focus in order to achieve clarity, positivity, and a clearer vision.

Mindfulness – an active state of mind when one engages in activities that are stimulating, fun, novel, and challenging. It is also experienced when a sense of spirit fills one up with joy and wonderment or deep connectedness.

Mindsight – an expression of interconnected emotions such as sympathy, empathy, concern, kindness, consideration, and care that reflect balance and integration of heart, body, and mind in response to everyday encounters.

Openness – willingness to consider any possibility.

Presence – ability to be attentive in the moment, in the here-and-now. At this point, all of one's senses are awakened.

Spiritual Embryo – an inherent force that pushes each newborn infant toward growth and development at the beginning of life.

Spirituality – the name of a complex system whereby love has ignited one's innate spiritual embryo so that deep connections and strong relationships have resulted in the development of a positive self of sense; where one's basic dispositions are touched by moments of wonderment, awe, joy, and/or inner peace; and where one's responses to the world include acts of caring, kindness, empathy, and/or reverence, that reflect one's inner complex dispositions. Qualities such as spiritual moments, caregiver love, mindfulness and mindsight, imagination, openness and acceptance, gratitude, and breath and presence are also important ingredients needed to nurture and sustain this system.

Spiritual-ness – a feeling of becoming or being filled with spirituality. It is the feeling one has when one experiences spiritual moments of wonderment, awe, joy, and inner peace. It is also experienced when one feels love, deep connections, and strong relationships, or when one acts with care, kindness, empathy, and/or reverence. Spiritual-ness is that which fills one up spiritually so that one can be a more caring and present person.

Spiritual Development –A system that begins with love and is supported by spiritual moments in time, space, nature, relationships, and big questions; nurtured by caregiver love, self-awareness, mindfulness and mindsight, imagination, openness and acceptance, gratitude, breath and presence; strengthened when one's basic dispositions are matched to wonder, awe, joy, and inner peace; and resulting in acts of caring, kindness, empathy, and reverence.

Wonderment – a feeling of surprise or amazement filled with quiet pause and reflection. Such feelings are stimulated by spiritual moments that connect to and strengthen one's basic dispositions.

© 2017 WHOLE PERSON ASSOCIATES, 101 WEST 2ND STREET, SUITE 203, DULUTH MN 55802 • 800-247-6789 • WHOLEPERSON.COM

Summary of Chapters

SECTION 1 – *Spiritual Moments*

Spiritual moments hold all the ingredients needed to begin the nurturing of spiritual development for both caregivers and children. Spiritual moments exist in time, in space, in and with nature, in relationships, and in confronting big questions that take one beyond oneself.

SECTION 2 – *Caregiver Love*

Caregiver love talks about the importance of love and attachments; ways love ignites the child's spiritual development, and how attachments lead children to feelings of connectedness, and eventually to the development of strong relationships.

SECTION 3 – *Self-Awareness*

When infants experience positive love and attachment they begin to develop a positive sense of self. In this way, young children begin a spiritual relationship with the world. Adults can also recapture a deeper sense of self-awareness by learning more about themselves and their own relationships with others and the world.

SECTION 4 – *Mindfulness and Mindsight*

Mindfulness connects to spiritual development by supporting one's ability to pause, take note, reflect, and appreciate novelty. Mindsight helps to integrate what one thinks, with how one acts. Together, mindfulness and mindsight describe the blending of heart, body, and mind, and help each of us to make good choices.

SECTION 5 – *Disposition*

The concept of disposition reflects a deep inner essence, a set of in-born passions present at birth in each one of us. This disposition must be nurtured in order to develop and maintain one's spirituality.

SECTION 6 – *Wonderment*

It is important to access one's own basic dispositions through feelings of wonderment, and then learn how to provide abundant moments of wonderment, awe, joy, and inner peace for oneself and for children.

SECTION 7– *Kindness*

Kindness is a complex disposition that includes benevolence, caring, compassion, consideration, empathy, generosity, helpfulness, and willingness to interact positively with others. This section discusses how complex dispositions guide our internal responses to external experiences.

(Continued on the next page)

© 2017 WHOLE PERSON ASSOCIATES, 101 WEST 2ND STREET, SUITE 203, DULUTH MN 55802 • 800-247-6789 • WHOLEPERSON.COM

Summary of Chapters (Continued)

SECTION 8 – ***Imagination***

Imagination invites spiritual development into one's life. Humor is an important quality for tapping into one's imagination.

SECTION 9 – *Openness & Acceptance*

By being open and accepting of all possibilities, one is able to strengthen one's spiritual self. Spiritual development becomes a part of one's life and a comfortable topic.

SECTION 10 – ***Gratitude***

Gratitude sweetens each moment. It heightens and guides one's spiritual moments for oneself and the children in one's life.

SECTION 11 – *Breath and Presence*

Caregivers can help children to bring themselves to each new situation in ways that reflect one's inner spiritual self. To do this, caregivers learn to model language and behavior that helps children be aware of their own breath and presence.

SECTION 12 – ***The BIG Picture: Spiritual Development***

All the components of spiritual development come together to be viewed and understood as a system.

Journaling

Many of the pages of this book will give you, the readers, the opportunity to journal responses to guided questions. This offers time and place to reflect, reminisce, be silent, think, and write about anything that comes to mind. The journaling process invites moments of reflection that help to tweak the brain in ways that encourage one to move forward. These journaling pages are just for you, or to be shared with those you trust. We wish you joy and wonderment in your life exploration to strengthen your own spiritual self and the spiritual development of the children you know.

© 2017 WHOLE PERSON ASSOCIATES, 101 WEST 2ND STREET, SUITE 203, DULUTH MN 55802 • 800-247-6789 • WHOLEPERSON.COM

Dedication

Several years ago I went back to my hometown of Cleveland, Ohio, and there was Deborah Schein! She came up to me excitedly and said "We need to write a book." It took months and months of talking together for me to understand the full concept of her vision and how it tied into the spiritual life I was clearly living. Writing this book has opened me up to even more avenues of spirituality than I knew existed. After co-writing workbooks about life skills, this book clearly took me out of my comfort zone and allowed me to delve into my own spiritual self. Deborah's friendship and guidance have been life-changing. Thanks Deb!

In the process of writing this book, I found a mentor. This mentor not only showed me how to write such a book, she guided and encouraged me to speak my own voice; to let go of the scholarly tone I had learned during my doctoral studies so that I might reach deep into my own experiences in order to share my own visions of spiritual development with her and with others who may read this book. I am forever indebted to Ester for this and for her patience, push, and deep concern for the readers. I now have new tools and a new venue in which to share this work. Thank you Ester!

We thank our husbands – Jay Leutenberg and Jeffrey Schein. Without their love and support, their constant and consistent care, this book would not exist. Our own spiritual development is deeply linked with theirs and we thank them with all our hearts.

We also dedicate this book to you, our readers. We wish you joy and wonderment on your quest to strengthen your own spiritual development and the spiritual development of the children you know.

Our thanks to the following professionals who make us look good!

Art Director – Mathew Pawlak
Editorial Director – Carlene Sippola
Illustrator – Amy Leutenberg Brodsky, LISW-S
Editor and Lifelong Teacher – Eileen Regen, MEd, CJE
Proofreader – Jay Leutenberg, CASA

Reviewers

Gene Bammel, PhD
Carol Butler Cooper, MS Ed, RN, C
Mickey Henson, MA
Amy Hirshberg Lederman, J.D, M.J.Ed.
Niki Tilicki, MA Ed

© 2017 WHOLE PERSON ASSOCIATES, 101 WEST 2ND STREET, SUITE 203, DULUTH MN 55802 • 800-247-6789 • WHOLEPERSON.COM

Table of Contents

(Continued on the next page)

© 2017 WHOLE PERSON ASSOCIATES, 101 WEST 2ND STREET, SUITE 203, DULUTH MN 55802 • 800-247-6789 • WHOLEPERSON.COM

Table of Contents *(Continued)*

© 2017 WHOLE PERSON ASSOCIATES, 101 WEST 2ND STREET, SUITE 203, DULUTH MN 55802 • 800-247-6789 • WHOLEPERSON.COM

Table of Contents (Continued)

© 2017 WHOLE PERSON ASSOCIATES, 101 WEST 2ND STREET, SUITE 203, DULUTH MN 55802 • 800-247-6789 • WHOLEPERSON.COM

SECTION I

Spiritual Moments

Spiritual Moments Happen Every Day

I was co-writing a book about spirituality, and on the way to a restaurant with friends, I asked the husband if he was religious, spiritual, spiritual and religious, or none of them. He gave me a confused look, and said, "What is spirituality?" I told him that it is different for everyone. I said, "For me, when I look at the mountains beyond my backyard, I have a sense of wonderment, of being a small part of the universe. It swells my heart." His response was, "I have no idea what you are talking about." We enjoyed our dinner, saying no more about it.

Driving home, he said he had been thinking. When he was at Machu Picchu, atop the Andes Mountains in Peru, he recalled an unbelievable feeling of awe. He reflected at that time upon his wonderment of the world. In the twenty-five minutes it took us to drive home, he told a half a dozen other stories like that. His wife's mouth was wide open. She, in fifty years of marriage, had never heard these stories. That one question opened him up to reflect and to recognize his spiritual moments and to consider his own spirituality.

~ Ester R.A. Leutenberg

© 2017 WHOLE PERSON ASSOCIATES, 101 WEST 2ND STREET, SUITE 203, DULUTH MN 55802 • 800-247-6789 • WHOLEPERSON.COM

Spiritual Moments in Time

Spiritual moments in time are quiet, calm moments with extended time for children to play and explore - these moments are most felt when children live their lives within a set routine and within environments that provide order. Such environments invite children to predict, know, and feel secure within a day, a week, or more.

Think about moments that have given you feelings of peace and contentment; moments when you felt as if time was simply stretched out before you and you had no need to hurry.

What are you doing in these reflective moments?

What ties these reflective moments together?

© 2017 WHOLE PERSON ASSOCIATES, 101 WEST 2ND STREET, SUITE 203, DULUTH MN 55802 • 800-247-6789 • WHOLEPERSON.COM

Spiritual Moments in Space

Spiritual moments in space describe young children's play environments that are aesthetically pleasing and beautiful; space where real objects, real experiences, and rich language are intentionally provided. This type of environment is often filled with moments of wonder, awe, joy, and inner peace that can fill each child's basic disposition.

Draw or describe what you would consider to be a beautiful learning space. What qualities would that space need?

© 2017 WHOLE PERSON ASSOCIATES, 101 WEST 2ND STREET, SUITE 203, DULUTH MN 55802 • 800-247-6789 • WHOLEPERSON.COM

Spiritual Moments in Relationships

Most children enjoy interactive relationships that are not stagnant, but that change in ways that stimulate their senses, intellect, and inner person. Such moments can help children to strengthen their will to self-regulate, be mindful, and take on responsibilities such as caring for a plant or garden, a pet, or helping to keep a room clean and organized.

We all have special people in our lives.

Referring to the above paragraph, think about the special people who were important to you as a young child. What made them so important to you?

Referring to that same paragraph, who are the special people in your life now and what makes them so important to you?

Describe how the qualities of the important people in your life, from your childhood to now, are the same or how they have changed.

© 2017 WHOLE PERSON ASSOCIATES, 101 WEST 2ND STREET, SUITE 203, DULUTH MN 55802 • 800-247-6789 • WHOLEPERSON.COM

Spiritual Moments in and with Nature

Many research studies have been conducted on nature's impact on human development. Kindness, respect, empathy, harmony, and being welcoming to others, are just a few of the benefits children engage in as they experience the natural world. As they explore the outdoors with nature, nature is also brought indoors for close-up exploration. Spiritual life begins with a sense of wonder, and one of the first windows leading to wonder is the natural world. In general, nature is an amazing source for wonder, awe, joy, inner-peace, and relationships. It eventually provides an environment for the emergence of big questions.

Go for a walk outdoors and look for moments that touch you spiritually.
Why do you think this is happening?
Try to put words to your feelings.

© 2017 WHOLE PERSON ASSOCIATES, 101 WEST 2ND STREET, SUITE 203, DULUTH MN 55802 • 800-247-6789 • WHOLEPERSON.COM

Spiritual Moments with Big Questions

Big questions are capable of taking one beyond oneself. When one engages in big questions, one is able to feel one's own place within the universe. If one believes in transcendence, then a big question can take the person to that place. If one does not, the big question can provide feelings of humility, smallness, and a feeling of a place within the vastness of the universe.

Young children are capable of big questions, also. You can see the question in a child's body posture, eyes, and expression. Through exploration of the world a myriad of questions come alive for a child. It is through big questions that a child is capable of seeing that the world exists way beyond oneself.

We all have big questions about life and how we see ourselves in the 'big picture'!

People often have big questions involving these aspects of life:

- Spiritual Moments
- Caregiver Love
- Self-Awareness
- Mindfulness and Mindsight
- Disposition
- Wonder
- Kindness
- Openness and Imagination
- Gratitude
- Breath and Presence
- The Big Picture: Spiritual Development

Although children may not be able to completely articulate their big questions, they hold curiosities and questions about how life works.

Examples might be:

- *Where does the sunlight come from?*
- *Why does light go away at night?*
- *Where do my shadows come from?*
- *Who creates a rainbow?*

An example of a big question from an adult might be:

- *What happens to a person when the person dies?*

A Big Question can lead you to explore spirituality from a personal perspective.

(Continued on the next page)

© 2017 WHOLE PERSON ASSOCIATES, 101 WEST 2ND STREET, SUITE 203, DULUTH MN 55802 • 800-247-6789 • WHOLEPERSON.COM

Spiritual Moments with Big Questions *(Continued)*

What is one of YOUR big questions about life in general that in some way involves one or more of the items listed on the prior page?

Why is this big question important to you?

© 2017 WHOLE PERSON ASSOCIATES, 101 WEST 2ND STREET, SUITE 203, DULUTH MN 55802 • 800-247-6789 • WHOLEPERSON.COM

The Relationship of Rituals and Spiritual Moments

A ritual is a ceremony or regular occurrence consisting of a series of actions performed according to a prescribed order and a set time. Some common rituals are saying good morning to someone when waking up, or singing a song to a child before going to bed. One's life is filled with rituals that strengthen one's spirituality.

What are some rituals that were shared with you as a child?

____

____

____

At the time, how did you feel about those rituals?

____

____

____

How did it make you feel to participate in those rituals?

____

____

____

How do rituals strengthen your spirituality?

____

____

____

What are some of the rituals you share with a child in your life?

____

____

____

© 2017 WHOLE PERSON ASSOCIATES, 101 WEST 2ND STREET, SUITE 203, DULUTH MN 55802 • 800-247-6789 • WHOLEPERSON.COM

Spiritual Moments: Thought-Provoking Quotations

"Spiritual moments happen every day. All you need to do is to know how and when to recognize them." ~ *Ester R.A. Leutenberg*

"Spiritual moments are created in relationships with others, in awareness and appreciation of self, in and with nature, and in dialogue with big questions capable of taking one beyond oneself." ~ *Deborah L. Schein*

After reading the above quotations, choose one and write your thoughts, create a poem, or draw a picture to describe your insights.

Quotation ____

© 2017 WHOLE PERSON ASSOCIATES, 101 WEST 2ND STREET, SUITE 203, DULUTH MN 55802 • 800-247-6789 • WHOLEPERSON.COM

Spiritual Moments

Ideas, Activities, and Moments for All Caregivers to Share with Children

Spiritual moments can sometimes happen by chance. More often, though, they need to be created by establishing nourishing connections. Here are some ways to provide spiritual moments for the children you know, and for yourself as well. Such moments can strengthen the spiritual development of everyone.

- Answer questions in a patient, thoughtful way.
- Ask the child to tell you a story. Then, ask questions about it.
- Breathe slowly with a young child, putting each of your hands on each other's heart.
- Clean up toys together.
- Create time in the day to simply be with the child.
- Dance together.
- Discuss the importance of friendship.
- Encourage quiet time.
- Enjoy reading with a child.
- Find a caterpillar and wonder together where it came from and what it will become.
- Find a spider's web and talk about it.
- Keep play spaces decluttered and organized, but expect them to get messed up.
- Laugh together.
- Limit saying *No* when you can – offer *Yes* or *Yes, but,* and don't be afraid to say no when it is truly needed.
- Look at the brown on a banana and together, wonder why it's there.
- Notice and discuss the wag of a dog's tail.
- Offer children time to play alone or with other children without any interruptions.
  Do not interfere.
  Do not show the child what to do.
  Do not suggest to the child to do something different than what the child has chosen to do.
  Do not talk.
- Pay attention to the environment, make it beautiful and inviting.
- Play together.
- See a shooting star, watch the moon, clouds, sunrise, or sunset.
- Show appreciation and respect when a child repeats something over and over again.
- Sing together.
- Stop and smell the roses.
- Support a child's right to have open time to play.
- Take time to answer children's questions.
- Talk about things for which to be grateful.
- Together, look at the shadows cast by the sun.
- Walk together.
- Watch and discuss a worm squiggling on the ground.
- When hearing a siren, say aloud, *We are wishing good thoughts to the person in the ambulance.*

Notes to Myself

(Thoughts and Ideas)

© 2017 WHOLE PERSON ASSOCIATES, 101 WEST 2ND STREET, SUITE 203, DULUTH MN 55802 • 800-247-6789 • WHOLEPERSON.COM

Things to Do

(Actions to Take)

SECTION 2

Caregiver Love

Love is the deep-seated emotion that gives us a feeling of connection.

After each feeding, I would burp my babies as recommended by the pediatrician. All three of my babies, in their own way, learned to reciprocate. Eventually, after a feeding and a burping, each baby would pat me on the back. The pats were gentle and rhythmic, similar to the pats I would give them. I will never know if they were simply mimicking my behavior, or if the babies really understood the value of an unspoken Thank You, and the return of love and care.

~ Deborah Schein

© 2017 WHOLE PERSON ASSOCIATES, 101 WEST 2ND STREET, SUITE 203, DULUTH MN 55802 • 800-247-6789 • WHOLEPERSON.COM

Caregiver Love

In this book, the term CAREGIVER refers to anyone GIVING CARE to a child: biological, adoptive, step, or foster parents; family members; child-care educators, day-care workers, and nannies.

This section explores the important role love plays in nurturing one's personal spiritual development and the spiritual development of young children.

Let's look first at the definition of love, the love a caregiver feels for a child. At a basic level, caregiver love is about affection, adoration, and devotion. It reflects an unconditional love required for healthy human development to occur. Those who are caregivers of infants know that this love is reciprocal. **Infants who are loved, love back.** There seems to be an invisible and unbreakable bond between infants and those who love them.

What have been your experiences with an infant and love? ______________________________

____

____

____

____

____

____

____

____

____

____

____

____

____

____

A child is born a spiritual being. It is the caregiver's responsibility to ignite spirituality with love. This creates an internal force that pushes the child to connect and develop meaningful relationships. These deep connections exist between an infant and others, with self, with nature, and with big questions capable of taking one beyond oneself. There is also a clear and important relationship between a child unconsciously feeling these connections and healthy learning and development.

© 2017 WHOLE PERSON ASSOCIATES, 101 WEST 2ND STREET, SUITE 203, DULUTH MN 55802 • 800-247-6789 • WHOLEPERSON.COM

Positive Attachment

Positive attachment is the bond created when love exists between the child and the caregiver. Both attachment and love provide balance between self and others. A young child who is lucky to experience deep love and attachment can begin to open up to the world and to others as relationships continue to increase and strengthen.

This type of love does not mean that a caregiver does absolutely everything for the child, or focuses solely on a child's happiness. Children need the opportunity to handle provocation and bumps along the way. Very young children are actually quite competent and capable. A loving caregiver offers children many opportunities to problem solve or to think of solutions through their own inquiry. This helps children learn to make good choices, explore the world, accept and appreciate differences, and develop awareness of the uniqueness of others.

The real focus is that of respecting children, including newborns, as people with valid and complex emotions, who need respect, understanding, and love.

Note your thoughts below about this quotation from Dr. Seuss.

A person's a person, no matter how small.

~ Dr. Seuss from *Horton Hears a Who!*

© 2017 WHOLE PERSON ASSOCIATES, 101 WEST 2ND STREET, SUITE 203, DULUTH MN 55802 • 800-247-6789 • WHOLEPERSON.COM

Personal Reflections on Your Own Love and Attachments

(If there is more than one person you wish to write about, photocopy and complete these two handouts for each person.)

As a young child, to whom do you remember feeling attached?

____

____

____

____

____

Was this the individual who cared for you and spent time with you at the beginning of your life? Explain.

____

____

____

____

____

What kind of memories do you have of this person?

____

____

____

____

____

(Continued on the next page)

© 2017 WHOLE PERSON ASSOCIATES, 101 WEST 2ND STREET, SUITE 203, DULUTH MN 55802 • 800-247-6789 • WHOLEPERSON.COM

Personal Reflections on Your Own Love and Attachments (Continued)

What memories do you have of yourself when you were with this person?

How did you feel when you spent time with this person?

Now think of a child with whom you feel a positive attachment and describe your love for this child.

How do you show your love in this relationship?

© 2017 WHOLE PERSON ASSOCIATES, 101 WEST 2ND STREET, SUITE 203, DULUTH MN 55802 • 800-247-6789 • WHOLEPERSON.COM

What Do You Know About Yourself

What do you know about yourself by having loved and having been loved?	What do you know about yourself by NOT having loved and NOT having been loved?

What do you need to do to be able to love and be loved? Who might be of help to you?

© 2017 WHOLE PERSON ASSOCIATES, 101 WEST 2ND STREET, SUITE 203, DULUTH MN 55802 • 800-247-6789 • WHOLEPERSON.COM

Caregiver Love: Thought-Provoking Quotations

"A person's most useful asset is not the head full of knowledge, but a heart full of love, an ear ready to listen, and a hand willing to help." ~ Anonymous

"There is something about being loved and protected by a parent [caregiver] knowing that I can be loved for who I am, not what I can do, or might one day become." ~ Jonathan Harnisch,

After reading the above quotations, choose one and write your thoughts, create a poem, or draw a picture to describe your insights.

Quotation ____

© 2017 WHOLE PERSON ASSOCIATES, 101 WEST 2ND STREET, SUITE 203, DULUTH MN 55802 • 800-247-6789 • WHOLEPERSON.COM

Caregiver Love

Ideas, Activities, and Moments for All Caregivers to Enjoy with Children

Love and attachment begin when caregivers are responsive to an infant's needs. This provides infants with feelings of trust, security, and safety that eventually provide a foundation for the development of self-awareness, relationships, learning, and an ability to experience continued spiritual development. A child's emotional needs are as important as a child's cognitive, social, physical, and spiritual needs.

- Accept and love the child no matter what the child's mood is.
- Be aware of your own body language as well as the child's body language.
- Be patient when the child is crying. Be calm and reassure that all is okay in the world.
- Be thoughtful and patient.
- Educate the child's heart.
- Engage in nonverbal emotional exchanges in ways that communicate the child's needs and make the child feel understood, secure, and balanced.
- Ensure that the child feels understood.
- Establish eye contact with love in your eyes.
- Give structure in order for the child to feel secure.
- Help a child find things and ideas to be passionate about.
- Hold and swing hands, not only because of safety, but because you are having fun.
- Look carefully for your child's disposition and honor it without trying to change it.
- Model compassion when a child's nonverbal cues tell you that he or she feels unhappy.
- Provide the child with needed kisses and hugs so the child feels loved.
- Randomly say, "I Love YOU!"
- Say what you mean and stick to it. Be consistent so the child can count on your word.
- Skip together when you are on a walk.
- Smile when you see the child.
- Spend quality time with the child.
- Think of every possible way to say "I love you!" Post-it notes in hiding places or in lunch boxes are fun.
- Using the word "no" appropriately can also say, "I love you" to the child.

© 2017 WHOLE PERSON ASSOCIATES, 101 WEST 2ND STREET, SUITE 203, DULUTH MN 55802 • 800-247-6789 • WHOLEPERSON.COM

Notes to Myself
(Thoughts and Ideas)

© 2017 WHOLE PERSON ASSOCIATES, 101 WEST 2ND STREET, SUITE 203, DULUTH MN 55802 • 800-247-6789 • WHOLEPERSON.COM

Things to Do

(Actions to Take)

Section 3

Self-Awareness

My Infants' Self-Awareness.

When my children were a few months old, my husband and I, would tie a piece of elastic onto one ankle of the baby. The other end of the elastic was tied to a mobile. (We would only do this when we had time to stay and watch; never leaving them alone tied to the mobile.) The babies each quickly noticed that when they kicked their foot, the mobile moved. They each slowly became aware that their leg was a part of their body and together, using mind and leg, the infants were able to move the mobile.

The recognition of physical self and the power it held became observable upon our three children's faces. It showed in their eyes and their body posture as alertness and a kind of awakening glimmered across their faces.

~ Deborah Schein

© 2017 WHOLE PERSON ASSOCIATES, 101 WEST 2ND STREET, SUITE 203, DULUTH MN 55802 • 800-247-6789 • WHOLEPERSON.COM

© 2017 WHOLE PERSON ASSOCIATES, 101 WEST 2ND STREET, SUITE 203, DULUTH MN 55802 • 800-247-6789 • WHOLEPERSON.COM

Self-Awareness

Self-awareness is a powerful outcome of positive love and positive attachment. It is also the next step in nurturing a young child's spiritual development. This section will discuss how self-awareness emerges directly from the spiritual embryo of a young child and how witnessing and sharing in this development can also strengthen the spirituality of adults who are responsible for nurturing and caring for young children.

When an infant is loved, two distinct feelings emerge to continue the construction of the infant's spiritual development. First there is a physical sense of self-awareness. Second, come feelings of deep interconnectedness, resulting in love of self and love of others.

Being loved creates in infants an unconscious sensation that there exists a "me"- the recipient of love. Infants unconsciously begin to feel, see, and perhaps think, *I am here. This is me. This skin, these hands, those toes, etc., are all a part of me.*

Think back to your childhood, or think about a child you might have watched grow up. What are some examples of a child's self-awareness?

(Continued on the next page)

© 2017 WHOLE PERSON ASSOCIATES, 101 WEST 2ND STREET, SUITE 203, DULUTH MN 55802 • 800-247-6789 • WHOLEPERSON.COM

Self-Awareness *(Continued)*

Infants also learn about love directly from the act of being loved. This represents the second outcome of positive love and secure attachment. It is an extension of self-worth that might evolve from feelings and thoughts such as "I am loved therefore I am loveable." Not only do loved children feel lovable, they also develop the capacity to love back. Researchers have discovered that this source of love can come from any important and consistent person in a child's life: a family member (parent, grandparent, aunt or uncle, sibling), caregiver, neighbor, or friend. The good news is that infants naturally seek out this type of emotional closeness.

In your experience, what are some acts of love that infants can sense? *(ex: kisses)*

In your experience, what are some ways that children return the love they receive? *(ex: smiles)*

© 2017 WHOLE PERSON ASSOCIATES, 101 WEST 2ND STREET, SUITE 203, DULUTH MN 55802 • 800-247-6789 • WHOLEPERSON.COM

Self-Awareness vs. Self-Esteem

What is the difference between self-awareness and self-esteem? The difference has to do with self and social connectedness. To some people it is about children's egocentricity and a perceived need that children need to be made to feel good about themselves. Unfortunately, too much self-esteem can lead to children needing and wanting to be the center of attention. This can eventually lead to unhealthy narcissism and possible seeds for bullying others.

Self-esteem is complex and changes as the child grows. It is not about "me," "mine," "my," but rather about the child developing a sense of self-worth that provides a foundation for becoming confident, yet sensitive to others.

Unfortunately, no matter how true this might be, it is only half the picture. Self-awareness, unlike self-esteem, is about awareness of self, people, and spaces, and therefore places the child into a social setting that involves connection to family, friends, culture, and community. Because of its popularity, a focus on self-esteem can influence a child to have an unhealthy amount of self-esteem and not enough self-awareness.

To further clarify self-esteem, one might picture a balloon filling up with so much air that it can burst. This would never happen with self-awareness. The more self-awareness one acquires, the more worldly and knowledgeable one becomes of self and of all that lives beyond oneself.

There is no such thing as too much self-awareness, but too much self-esteem can lead to feelings of entitlement. An entitled human being often acts without the benefit or ability to make wise choices based upon a shared value system. Someone with too much self-esteem might also be considered as egocentric.

While awareness leads to more understanding and connectedness, in some cases, the more self-esteem one acquires, the more entitled one can feel. Without having the ability to make wise choices based upon a wise value system, self-esteem can lead to egocentric behavior.

How would you describe your self-esteem?

____

____

____

How would you describe your self-awareness?

____

____

____

Which supports you in making meaningful connections with other people, and with the world in general, self-esteem or self-awareness? Explain.

____

____

____

____

© 2017 WHOLE PERSON ASSOCIATES, 101 WEST 2ND STREET, SUITE 203, DULUTH MN 55802 • 800-247-6789 • WHOLEPERSON.COM

Praise

Educators and parents who believe that children are egocentric, sometime try to build up their children's self-esteem with praise. Building a child's self-esteem with an over-abundance of praise can lead children to feelings of insecurity and pressure.

Children do need praise, but the kind of praise and for what purpose, may have a profound effect on young children's development of their sense-of-self. Praise should be meaningful, specific, and authentic without exaggeration. Appropriate and proper praise requires that caregivers closely and purposefully observe children to glean an understanding of each child.

Each child's uniqueness is evident through behavior, language, body posture, choices, etc. Each child also brings a variety of strengths and weaknesses in responses to the world which are also influenced by birth order, interests, and brain development. As a child's many nuances become known to caregivers, it becomes more apparent when and how to praise a child.

Appropriate praise can help to build a child's self-awareness, however, inappropriate praise can lead to a distorted self-esteem.

What is an example of appropriate praise to a child?

(ex: I like the way you take responsibility for cleaning your room!)

____

____

____

____

What is an example of inappropriate praise that can lead to a distorted self-esteem?

(ex: Everything you do is perfect! or: You will be able to do anything you want to!)

____

____

____

____

How would you keep self-esteem and praise in check?

(ex: Think first about what I really want to say.)

____

____

____

____

© 2017 WHOLE PERSON ASSOCIATES, 101 WEST 2ND STREET, SUITE 203, DULUTH MN 55802 • 800-247-6789 • WHOLEPERSON.COM

Intra-Personal Intelligence and Inter-Personal Intelligence

There are differences in children's natural intelligences: intra-personal intelligence, through which the child has a clear focus towards self, and inter-personal intelligence, through which the focus is directed toward others. Together, intra-personal intelligence and inter-personal intelligence support a child's developing sense of self-awareness and connectedness that simultaneously support the child's spiritual development.

What is an example of your own intra-personal intelligence? (A clear focus towards yourself.)

**What is an example of your own inter-personal intelligence?
(The focus is directed toward others.).**

How can both of these combined be an asset to you?

How can both of these combined be an asset to a child?

Eventually this foundation supports children's sense of inner security and leads to their ability to look outward toward new experiences, relationships, and questions. These same experiences also strengthen the intra-personal intelligence of the child with self-awareness. This ability to look outward opens a child's relationship to the world and many moments of wonder, awe, joy, and inner peace. These experiences promote the development of the child's spiritual life.

© 2017 WHOLE PERSON ASSOCIATES, 101 WEST 2ND STREET, SUITE 203, DULUTH MN 55802 • 800-247-6789 • WHOLEPERSON.COM

Developing Spiritual Practices for Self-Awareness

Self-awareness is a powerful outcome of positive love and positive attachment. It emerges from a child's spiritual embryo as each child grows in personal awareness of physical self. The child realizes that there is a "me" and this "me" has ability to feel deeply connected to others. This realization, be it conscious or not, is the beginning step toward forming relationships and produces within the child a growing love of self and an ability to love others.

Some guidelines for understanding and nurturing self-awareness in young children:

- A child's self-awareness begins with being and feeling loved. Simply and authentically bestow love upon your child.
- Use appropriate kisses, hugs, and smiles to demonstrate your affection for the child.
- If and when you praise a child, make it authentic and meaningful to the child. Too much praise can indirectly create pressure and insecurity resulting in weakening a child's sense of self.
- Help children find a balance between relationships with self and others by recognizing both of these sides of self: intra-personal and inter-personal intelligence. Intra-personal reflects self-knowledge and inter-personal refers to relationships.
- Provide some balance between time alone and time with others.
- Provide suggestions for developing self-awareness of children and ways to avoid the dangers of too much self-esteem or centeredness. Young children are not usually egocentric when inter-awareness is nurtured.
- Don't be afraid to move beyond a child's preference as we also want children to develop resiliency. But, do this respectfully.

  What to say: "I know you like to sleep in a dark room but today there is light coming in through the window. I think you might like it. Why don't you give it a try?"

  If we view all children as competent, then challenges must also become part of the dialogue. Taking on a doable challenge can eventually lead to new strengths, growth, and development.

  Such challenges are built into human development.

What might you say to support an infant's growing sense of self? Focus on using the language of self-awareness instead of self-esteem to help children reach their full potential. What not to say.

Focus on using the language of self-awareness instead of self-esteem to help children reach their full potential.	What not to say.
"Look at you. You rolled over."	"Good job!" *Not specific enough*
"You are getting stronger."	"Good boy." or "Good girl." *Connects child's self to accomplishments*
"Are you going to try again?'	"You are the best baby in the world." *Not relational*

Life is filled with internal and external challenges and caregivers can be an infant's support and cheerleader. But the real work is accomplished by the child within relationships.

A thought about the word *best*: It is a word worthy of avoiding. If we remember that all other children are going through the same developmental processes, each in their own way, then the only true comparison can be to oneself. On the other hand, the word *best* implies one has arrived at a place that cannot be surpassed. If we think of learning and development as lifelong accomplishments, then the word *best* cannot really exist within this framework.

The word *best* brings on unneeded and sometimes unwanted competition. The challenge should be internal so that each child moves forward based upon personal interests, competencies, and desired or needed areas for growth.

© 2017 WHOLE PERSON ASSOCIATES, 101 WEST 2ND STREET, SUITE 203, DULUTH MN 55802 • 800-247-6789 • WHOLEPERSON.COM

Self-Awareness: Thought-Provoking Quotations

"The greatest thing in the world is to know how to belong to oneself." ~ Michel de Montaigne

"At the center of your being you have the answer; you know who you are and you know what you want." ~ Lao Tzu

After reading the above quotations, choose one and write your thoughts, create a poem, or draw a picture to describe your insights.

Quotation ____

Self-Awareness

Ideas, Activities, and Moments for All Caregivers to Enjoy with Children

A child's self-awareness is built upon parents' or caregivers' love and the child's growing ability to have relationships that promote self-awareness.

- Acknowledge new accomplishments.
- Be a good listener.
- Create opportunities for the child to decide when playtime is over, at least some of the time.
- Don't be afraid to give feedback if and when it is needed.
- Encourage playing alone as well as playing with others.
- Help the child to express personal feelings.
- It is okay to have a good cry along with the child.
- Make sure that the child has a variety of experiences.
- Mimic a young child's sounds and expressions. This will help the child mimic yours.
- Offer praise when warranted, but don't overdo.
- Pay attention to the words you say to the child.

  Do's and Don'ts:
  - Do not continually say "No."
  - Do say, "Look at you ________" rather than "You are the best ________."
  - Do say, "You are ________" Rather than "good boy" or "good girl."
  - Do say, "You gave it your all by ________" rather than "good job" without specifics.
- Place the child in front of a mirror to learn about self.
- Present opportunities for the child to make choices.
- Promote interaction with other adults.
- Provide play dates with other children.
- Put the child in front of you for the child to see self in your eyes.
- See and appreciate each child for specific attributes.
- Show interest by answering the child's questions.
- Smile at accomplishments.
- Support friendship and bonding with other children.
- Help the child to see the funny side of a not-so-funny situation.
- Think self-awareness not self-esteem
- Use the infant's name so the infant will identify with it.
- Watch carefully and notice the child's likes and dislikes.

© 2017 WHOLE PERSON ASSOCIATES, 101 WEST 2ND STREET, SUITE 203, DULUTH MN 55802 • 800-247-6789 • WHOLEPERSON.COM

Notes to Myself

(Thoughts and Ideas)

© 2017 WHOLE PERSON ASSOCIATES, 101 WEST 2ND STREET, SUITE 203, DULUTH MN 55802 • 800-247-6789 • WHOLEPERSON.COM

Things to Do

(Actions to Take)

© 2017 WHOLE PERSON ASSOCIATES, 101 WEST 2ND STREET, SUITE 203, DULUTH MN 55802 • 800-247-6789 • WHOLEPERSON.COM

SECTION 4

Mindfulness and Mindsight

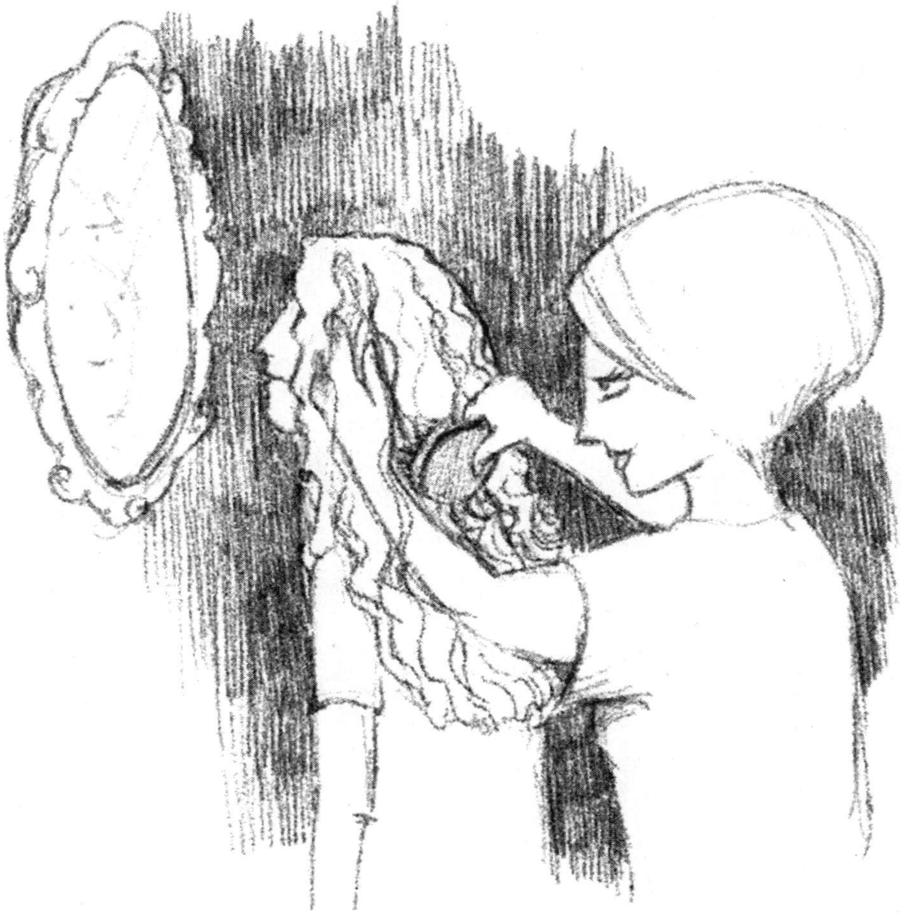

A Mindful Lesson Learned from a Child

My eldest daughter had long, curly, snarly, beautiful strawberry blonde hair as a child. One day, when she was fairly young, I was brushing her hair and upset with her older brother at the same time. With every angry statement coming out of my mouth to him, my hand was apparently brushing with the same anger.

My daughter said to me, "You know Mom, just because you are angry at someone else, doesn't mean you should take it out on my head!" It was truly a poignant, important lesson learned – to pause, enjoy the mother-daughter moment, and later, gather my thoughts, get my emotions under control, and have a meaningful discussion with my son.

~ Ester Leutenberg

© 2017 WHOLE PERSON ASSOCIATES, 101 WEST 2ND STREET, SUITE 203, DULUTH MN 55802 • 800-247-6789 • WHOLEPERSON.COM

© 2017 WHOLE PERSON ASSOCIATES, 101 WEST 2ND STREET, SUITE 203, DULUTH MN 55802 • 800-247-6789 • WHOLEPERSON.COM

Mindfulness

As children continue to develop the sense of self, they are also able to grow in their ability to be mindful.

Mindfulness can be equated with spiritualness – the sense of spirit that fills each person. It has both an active and passive side. Mindfulness is an active state of mind found when one engages in activities that are stimulating, fun, interesting, or even provocative, novel, or challenging. It also refers to calm and quiet moments that help one reconnect to self and increase one's ability to use one's senses and to make thoughtful decisions.

Mindsight involves interactive emotions that connect one to other emotions such as sympathy, empathy, concern, kindness, consideration, and care. In the process of experiencing mindsight, individuals may also feel integrative harmony both internally and externally. This is to say that balance between heart, body, and mind is achieved so that one not only feels good inside, but also acts compassionately in response to everyday encounters.

One way to nurture mindfulness and mindsight is through the practice of meditation.

Meditation is a process by which one encourages and develops a deeper ability to concentrate and focus in order to achieve clarity, positivity, and a true vision of the nature of things.

A Meditation Exercise

Focus your attention on your breath, the inhale and exhale.

Sit or lie in a comfortable position.

Maintain your focus by closing your eyes.

Take an exaggerated breath: a deep inhale through your nostrils, hold your breath for a couple of seconds, and a long exhale through your mouth.

Focus on the rise and fall of your chest or the sensation through your nostrils.

If your mind wanders as you are distracted by thoughts or bodily sensations, just notice that this is happening and gently bring your attention back to your breath.

© 2017 WHOLE PERSON ASSOCIATES, 101 WEST 2ND STREET, SUITE 203, DULUTH MN 55802 • 800-247-6789 • WHOLEPERSON.COM

Mindfulness, Mindsight, and You

How does **mindfulness** apply to your life? *(ex: I try to stay in the here-and-now.)*.

What do you do to support this mindfulness? *(ex: I will pause before taking action.)*

How does **mindsight** apply to your life? *(ex: When I go for a walk, I come back feeling whole.)*

What do you do to support this mindsight? *(ex: I use mindfulness, pause, and appreciation.)*

Describe ways Mindfulness and Mindsight reflect your Spirituality.

© 2017 WHOLE PERSON ASSOCIATES, 101 WEST 2ND STREET, SUITE 203, DULUTH MN 55802 • 800-247-6789 • WHOLEPERSON.COM

Mindful Practices for the Caregiver

How do you, or can you, model a life filled with mindfulness and mindsight?

Mindful and Mindsight Practices	Your Thoughts …
Allow a special time to let your mind wander, or not, depending on what you need.	
Be conscientious about what is good for your body.	
Be conscientious of what you put in your mind.	
Beauty is everywhere – take time to see it.	
Commit to writing reflections in your journal.	
Go out in nature, no matter what the weather.	
Journal your reflections on a regular basis.	
Invite newness and novelty into your life.	
Let yourself feel what you're feeling.	
Live and enjoy each moment - take time to slow down and notice your surroundings.	
Share your appreciation with the people in your life.	
Take time to meditate.	
Take time to notice small details every day by using your sight, sound, smell, taste, and touch.	
To avoid distractions, stay present and in the moment.	
Uni-task – not multi-task – so you can feel each moment.	
Use your smart phone in a smart way. Don't let it take over your life.	
Wake up ready for a new day.	
When listening to someone, listen with your whole self.	
When tense, just breathe.	
When your mind wanders, bring it back, or let it wander, depending on what you need.	

© 2017 WHOLE PERSON ASSOCIATES, 101 WEST 2ND STREET, SUITE 203, DULUTH MN 55802 • 800-247-6789 • WHOLEPERSON.COM

Mindfulness: Thought-Provoking Quotations

"Mind is a flexible mirror. Adjust it to see a better world." ~ *Amit Ray*

"Mindfulness is simply being aware of what is happening right now without wishing it were different; enjoying the pleasant without holding on when it changes (which it will); being with the unpleasant without fearing it will always be this way (which it won't.)" ~ *James Baraz*

After reading the above quotations, choose one and write your thoughts, create a poem, or draw a picture to describe your insights.

Quotation ____

 © 2017 WHOLE PERSON ASSOCIATES, 101 WEST 2ND STREET, SUITE 203, DULUTH MN 55802 • 800-247-6789 • WHOLEPERSON.COM

Mindfulness and Mindsight

Ideas, Activities, and Moments for All Caregivers to Share with Children

As children continue to develop the sense of self, they are also able to grow in their ability to be mindful. Mindfulness can be equated with spiritual-ness – it is the sense of mindfulness of spirit that fills us. With children, mindsight (integration of heart, mind, and body) will emerge. Below are some ways to understand and nurture the spiritual side of young children.

- Ask the child to stare at an object for a minute or two and then, draw it.
- At an early age, meditate in front of the child, and after a while, invite him or her to meditate with you.
- Create surprises for children:
  - For play:
    - Add a few marbles in a bowl of rocks.
    - Add a few pebbles in a bowl of beads.
  - At home:
    - Add a few grapes in a bowl of blueberries.
- Demonstrate to a child how to notice one's surroundings.
- Go slowly – teach thoughtfulness.
- Help the child to pay close attention to a tree, a flower, a leaf, etc.
- Listen to the child with interest, without being distracted or looking away.
- Model laughing at yourself, but never at others.
- Notice together:
  - A gaggle of geese flying through the sky.
  - A plant pushing through the sidewalk.
- Pay attention to how your breath feels, sounds, and looks as you breathe in and out together.
- Pick up someone else's litter, or your own, and throw it in a trash can with the help of the child.
- Request that the child closes eyes. Put an orange, sea shell, rock, etc., in front of the child. Ask the child to smell, touch, or feel, and guess what it is.
- Run outside with the child. Stop. Pay attention to hearts beating and then hearts slowing down.
- See the humorous things in life and laugh a lot with the child.
- Sit still with a child in a still, serene, natural setting.
- Take time with a child to each hold a beautiful rock in your hands.
- Teach gratitude by noticing together the things you have to be grateful for.
- Tread lightly while watching the child play. Be helpful without offering too much direction or any judgments.

© 2017 WHOLE PERSON ASSOCIATES, 101 WEST 2ND STREET, SUITE 203, DULUTH MN 55802 • 800-247-6789 • WHOLEPERSON.COM

Notes to Myself

(Thoughts and Ideas)

© 2017 WHOLE PERSON ASSOCIATES, 101 WEST 2ND STREET, SUITE 203, DULUTH MN 55802 • 800-247-6789 • WHOLEPERSON.COM

Things to Do

(Actions to Take)

SECTION 5

Disposition

Discovering a Child's Disposition

My youngest daughter was the baby of four children. At the age of two she showed an exceptional talent for art. At dinner, her brother and sisters excitedly chatted about the daily school happenings. She wanted to participate but wasn't attending school and had nothing new to offer.

However - it seemed so clear to me that she had an amazing talent – her artwork. At age of 3, we hired a high school student to come to our home once a week to give her art lessons for an hour. She began to bring her pictures to the dinner table and we all connected with her, and she with us, through her artwork.

We are each born with an inner disposition. To know it and to nurture it helps us to feel complete, whole, and unique.

~ Ester Leutenberg

© 2017 WHOLE PERSON ASSOCIATES, 101 WEST 2ND STREET, SUITE 203, DULUTH MN 55802 • 800-247-6789 • WHOLEPERSON.COM

© 2017 WHOLE PERSON ASSOCIATES, 101 WEST 2ND STREET, SUITE 203, DULUTH MN 55802 • 800-247-6789 • WHOLEPERSON.COM

What is Disposition?

A disposition is similar to one's personality or passions but much deeper and much more connected to one's inner self. Disposition is that internal something that dictates favorite color, foods, and choices of activities. Basic dispositions are internal feelings triggered by moments of wonder, awe, joy, and inner peace. Complex dispositions are reflected in how one acts towards another person by caring and showing kindness, empathy, and reverence. One's dispositions guide a person sometimes unknowingly through life. They act as a guiding internal force that stays within each person, sometimes unrecognized, through life. If one is lucky, it may lead to a lifetime profession and/or to an interest that often becomes one's life's passion.

As a child, what were your passions?

____

____

____

How did the adults in your life respond to those passions?

____

____

____

How did this make you feel?

____

____

____

How have those childhood passions continued or changed?

____

____

____

© 2017 WHOLE PERSON ASSOCIATES, 101 WEST 2ND STREET, SUITE 203, DULUTH MN 55802 • 800-247-6789 • WHOLEPERSON.COM

Passions

When one's passions (dispositions) are not recognized, supported, and nurtured, one's sense of self or one's self-awareness may be jeopardized. Nurturing one's disposition helps one to open up to new situations and helps one to learn important things about oneself.

What are your passions today?

____

____

____

____

Describe how it feels when you share your passions with others.

____

____

____

____

How do you nurture passions for children?

____

____

____

____

What might happen when children's dispositions are not shared or nurtured, but are mis-read, ignored, or even worse, thwarted.

____

____

____

____

As adults, it is our responsibility to nurture children's passions (dispositions)!

© 2017 WHOLE PERSON ASSOCIATES, 101 WEST 2ND STREET, SUITE 203, DULUTH MN 55802 • 800-247-6789 • WHOLEPERSON.COM

Basic Dispositions

In the system of spiritual development, when a child's disposition is nurtured, the child feels amazing moments of wonder, awe, joy, and inner peace. These feelings can naturally set the stage for the emergence of pro-social behaviors. Think about it. When you are filled with joy, don't you want to be more kind and caring toward others? This leads to spiritual development which can naturally emerge if children's dispositions are nurtured.

Character development naturally emerges from a child's disposition and the environment in which the child lives. Positive role modeling is an effective means of guiding development of a child's character. .

In what ways, and how, do you model character development, disposition, and passions for children?

Disposition is the predominant or prevailing tendency of one's spirits.

© 2017 WHOLE PERSON ASSOCIATES, 101 WEST 2ND STREET, SUITE 203, DULUTH MN 55802 • 800-247-6789 • WHOLEPERSON.COM

Disposition: Thought-Provoking Quotations

"Disposition is something deep within us that identifies who we are." ~ *Deborah Schein*

"Knowing our own dispositions help us to recognize our children's dispositions." ~ *Ester Leutenberg*

After reading the above quotations, choose one and write your thoughts, create a poem, or draw a picture to describe your insights.

Quotation ____

© 2017 WHOLE PERSON ASSOCIATES, 101 WEST 2ND STREET, SUITE 203, DULUTH MN 55802 • 800-247-6789 • WHOLEPERSON.COM

Disposition

Ideas, Activities, and Moments for All Caregivers to Share with Children

Below are ways for you to become more aware of the child's disposition or innate self. Once you see it, continue to encourage what the child likes and enjoys. Observe the ways the child displays talents while simultaneously introducing the child to new experiences.

- Know the child well enough to have appropriate props available to play.
- Offer the child time to engage in activities of choice.
- Recognize, respect, support, and name the child's unique dispositions.
- Remember that each child is unique.
- Smile when the child finds a passion.
- Spend quality time in spiritual moments with the child.
- Support the child's imagination.
- Support the child's right to have open time to play.
- Use varied modes of expression that speak to the child.
- Wonder together about everything that catches the attention of both you and the child.

Try these different ways to discover your child's disposition and give the child encouragement, time, space, and support to engage in these activities.

Notice … Acknowledge … Observe …
- Animals, birds, turtles, etc.
- Colors
- Insects in the garden and in picture books
- Leaves, acorns, bark, flowers, seashells, stones, rocks, etc
- Shadows
- Stars, moon, constellations in the night sky
- Temperatures
- Textures

Provide …
- Choices of trying different sports
- Materials for art: chalk, paint, paper, pens, odd junk, etc.
- Music and movement time
- Opportunities for play in the sand, mud, water, snow, rain, etc.
- Picture and story books

© 2017 WHOLE PERSON ASSOCIATES, 101 WEST 2ND STREET, SUITE 203, DULUTH MN 55802 • 800-247-6789 • WHOLEPERSON.COM

Notes to Myself

(Thoughts and Ideas)

© 2017 WHOLE PERSON ASSOCIATES, 101 WEST 2ND STREET, SUITE 203, DULUTH MN 55802 • 800-247-6789 • WHOLEPERSON.COM

Things to Do

(*Actions to Take*)

Wonderment

Summer Flowers and Music Bring Shared Wonderment

One summer night while listening to a summer outdoor band concert I witnessed two lively little girls. One was around two years old, the other maybe three. As they approached the band stage, the little one saw a lovely pot of pink flowers. She was immediately drawn to them. Just then, her older friend began dancing … swinging arms, moving hips, picking up feet, tossing her head. Her entire body was engaged in movement and music. The draw was stronger than the pretty flowers and before long both girls were dancing away.

When I looked again, the little one was no longer dancing. Her disposition was so strong that she was now picking small flowers and handing them to her dad who was keeping her treasures in a small cup. Not only was this little girl picking flowers but so was her friend and a few other children attending the concert.

A child's disposition can have a strong pull upon a child and is even better when shared and supported during moments of wonderment. The smallest girl came with a disposition and love of flowers and she succeeded, possibly with the help of her father, to share her passion with others. Together, all the children were able to experience moments of wonderment by spending time in nature, seeing and smelling the beautiful flowers, working together to make a collection, and simply being together on a lovely summer evening.

Later, the girls returned to dancing (possibly another source of wonderment) and so the evening went. Both girls left with their parents and they were satisfied with their activities and ready for bed.

~ Deborah Schein

© 2017 WHOLE PERSON ASSOCIATES, 101 WEST 2ND STREET, SUITE 203, DULUTH MN 55802 • 800-247-6789 • WHOLEPERSON.COM

© 2017 WHOLE PERSON ASSOCIATES, 101 WEST 2ND STREET, SUITE 203, DULUTH MN 55802 • 800-247-6789 • WHOLEPERSON.COM

Moments of Wonderment, Awe, and Joy

When individuals know their own disposition, or when a caregiver realizes a child's disposition, then that disposition can be filled with moments of wonderment. Feelings of wonderment are produced when people spend time in spiritual moments with self and others, space, time, and nature, or by asking big important questions in ways that move them spiritually. Such feelings are deeply and internally felt and most often occur when one experiences spiritual moments.

Sometimes a spiritual moment happens spontaneously. Other times, one can actually provide an environment that is capable of creating such moments. Moments of wonderment often occur when one spends time in and with nature.

Caregivers of young children must look at ways to create personal moments of wonderment. Everyone needs time – time to be alone – and time to explore, play, think, feel grateful, and ponder. In this state of being, one can also learn more about self and personal connectedness to all in the environment. It is possible to open oneself up to new connections, fresh ideas, different ways of thinking and knowing by embracing new experiences that provide wonderment, awe, and joy.

Honoring one's disposition means spending time within spiritual moments so that one's spirit can be felt. When one feels these inner feelings, often defined as wonderment, joy, or awe, life is generally seen as good, even if and when bad things happen.

We have the power to make ourselves feel worthy of life.

When we are able to feel wonderment,
we can also create opportunities for children to feel wonderment, awe, and joy.

In response to the statements below, use the examples to stimulate your own reflections.

Reflect on some of your past moments of wonderment. *(ex: Birth of my first child.)*

____

____

Reflect on some of your past moments of awe. *(ex: When my child recognized me.)*

____

____

Reflect on some of your past moments of joy. *(ex: When my child smiled at me.)*

____

____

© 2017 WHOLE PERSON ASSOCIATES, 101 WEST 2ND STREET, SUITE 203, DULUTH MN 55802 • 800-247-6789 • WHOLEPERSON.COM

What Kind of Space?

What kind of space provides you with wonderment? *(ex: Looking out at the mountains.)* ______________________

____

____

____

____

What kind of space provides you with awe? *(ex: Noticing the vastness of the mountains.)* ______________________

____

____

____

____

What kind of space provides you with joy? *(ex: How happy I am when hiking on the trails.)* ______________________

____

____

____

____

What kind of space provides wonderment for a child in your life? ______________________

____

____

____

____

What kind of space provides awe for a child in your life? ______________________

____

____

____

____

What kind of space provides joy for a child in your life? ______________________

____

____

____

____

© 2017 WHOLE PERSON ASSOCIATES, 101 WEST 2ND STREET, SUITE 203, DULUTH MN 55802 • 800-247-6789 • WHOLEPERSON.COM

What Kind of Time?

What kind of time provides you with wonderment? *(ex: The weekends.)* ______________________

What kind of time provides you with awe? *(ex: How it fulfills me and prepares me for the week.)* ______________________

What kind of time provides you with joy? *(ex: Choosing and planning activities that are satisfying.)* ______________________

What kind of time provides wonderment for a child in your life? ______________________

What kind of time provides awe for a child in your life? ______________________

What kind of time provides joy for a child in your life? ______________________

© 2017 WHOLE PERSON ASSOCIATES, 101 WEST 2ND STREET, SUITE 203, DULUTH MN 55802 • 800-247-6789 • WHOLEPERSON.COM

What Kind of People?

What kind of people provide you with wonderment? *(ex: Children.)*

What kind of people provide you with awe? *(ex: Children who are not afraid to try something new.)*

What kind of people provide you with joy? *(ex: Children I connect with.)*

What kind of people provide wonderment for a child in your life?

What kind of people provide awe for a child in your life?

What kind of people provide joy for a child in your life?

© 2017 WHOLE PERSON ASSOCIATES, 101 WEST 2ND STREET, SUITE 203, DULUTH MN 55802 • 800-247-6789 • WHOLEPERSON.COM

What About Nature?

What aspects of nature provide you with wonderment? *(ex: Watching my pumpkins grow.)* ________________

What aspects of nature provide you with awe? *(ex: Seeing the first sprout of the seed.)*________________

What aspects of nature provide you with joy? *(ex: Harvesting and roasting pumpkin seeds.)*________________

What aspects of nature provide wonderment for a child in your life?________________

What aspects of nature provide awe for a child in your life? ________________

What aspects of nature provide joy for a child in your life? ________________

© 2017 WHOLE PERSON ASSOCIATES, 101 WEST 2ND STREET, SUITE 203, DULUTH MN 55802 • 800-247-6789 • WHOLEPERSON.COM

What About Being Connected?

What kind of connections provide you with wonderment? *(ex: I feel lucky to have children in my life.)*

What kind of connections provide you with awe? *(ex: When children are capable of cheering me up.)*

What kind of connections provide you with joy? *(ex: Sharing a new experience with children.)*

What kind of connections provide wonderment for a child in your life?

What kind of connections provide awe for a child in your life?

What kind of connections provide joy for a child in your life?

© 2017 WHOLE PERSON ASSOCIATES, 101 WEST 2ND STREET, SUITE 203, DULUTH MN 55802 • 800-247-6789 • WHOLEPERSON.COM

What Kind of Big Questions?

What kind of big questions provide you with wonderment? *(ex: How did I become me?)*

What kind of big questions provide you with awe? *(ex: Why am I here?)*

What kind of big questions provide you with joy? *(ex: What do I have to look forward to?)*

What kind of big questions provide wonderment for a child in your life?

What kind of big questions provide awe for a child in your life?

What kind of big questions provide joy for a child in your life?

© 2017 WHOLE PERSON ASSOCIATES, 101 WEST 2ND STREET, SUITE 203, DULUTH MN 55802 • 800-247-6789 • WHOLEPERSON.COM

Wonderment: Thought-Provoking Quotations

"Give yourself a gift of five minutes of contemplation in awe of everything you see around you. Go outside and turn your attention to the many miracles around you …" ~ *Wayne Dyer*

"Never stop wandering into wonder." ~ *Suzy Kassem*

After reading the above quotations, choose one and write your thoughts, create a poem, or draw a picture to describe your insights.

Quotation ____

© 2017 WHOLE PERSON ASSOCIATES, 101 WEST 2ND STREET, SUITE 203, DULUTH MN 55802 • 800-247-6789 • WHOLEPERSON.COM

Wonderment

Ideas, Activities, and Moments for All Caregivers to Share with Children

Feeling moments of wonder brings us to a place where each of us is capable of feeling a deeper sense of being. This is how our spiritual side is brought forward through the use of all of our senses . . . WE FEEL! We feel wonder, awe, joy, and inner peace as we connect with the world. One's disposition is also in play because not everything produces wondrous moments for everyone. Find your wonder and help children find theirs.

- Appreciate the awesomeness of a rainbow.
- Be aware of the wonders of the world yourself in order to pass them along to the child.
- Develop a loving and trusting relationship with the child.
- Collect amazing objects while going for a walk.
- Educate the child's heart by spending time together and also giving the child space to be alone.
- Experience with the child the wonder of a small pebble, a large boulder, and other extremes in nature.
- Find appreciation and joy in all relationships and share this with the child.
- Go outside and watch the sunrise or sunset.
- Introduce the child to reflective properties found in water and glass.
- Listen to a sea shell.
- Look at the colors and cloud formations in the sky.
- Notice the emergence of a flower from a seed, to a tiny green shoot, to leaves, to a bud, to a flower.
- Observe the breathing of a sleeping baby.
- Play music and sway to the beat. Share this moment with the child.
- See a spider spin a web.
- Start a garden together. Share moments of change with the child, plant a seed, and watch it sprout.
- Show appreciation of nature by taking a walk in the park and observe different leaves, bark, etc.
- Spot a rainbow and talk about it.
- Take a picture of an awesome sight, look at it, and talk about it with the child.
- Together, watch an ant creep across the sidewalk.
- Use a telescope and look at the stars. Wonder together how they got up there.
- Watch a thunderstorm through the window.
- With a microscope, look at an egg shell or anything else that appeals to the child.

© 2017 WHOLE PERSON ASSOCIATES, 101 WEST 2ND STREET, SUITE 203, DULUTH MN 55802 • 800-247-6789 • WHOLEPERSON.COM

Notes to Myself

(Thoughts and Ideas)

© 2017 WHOLE PERSON ASSOCIATES, 101 WEST 2ND STREET, SUITE 203, DULUTH MN 55802 • 800-247-6789 • WHOLEPERSON.COM

Things to Do

(Actions to Take)

© 2017 WHOLE PERSON ASSOCIATES, 101 WEST 2ND STREET, SUITE 203, DULUTH MN 55802 • 800-247-6789 • WHOLEPERSON.COM

SECTION 7

Kindness

Feeling Kindness

I had a teddy bear – Smokey the Bear to be exact. He came with a shovel, a hat, and a belt with his name on it. I kept Smokey throughout my life, and when I recently moved, I asked my grandchildren (ages five and seven) if I should keep him or let him go. Without hesitation they answered, "Keep him Grandma!" It didn't matter at all to them that Smokey was old and falling apart. They understood that if I had kept this toy for this long, then it must be very important to me. Each one then offered me one of their own very special stuffed animals just in case Smokey didn't make it through the big move.

~ Deborah Schein

© 2017 WHOLE PERSON ASSOCIATES, 101 WEST 2ND STREET, SUITE 203, DULUTH MN 55802 • 800-247-6789 • WHOLEPERSON.COM

© 2017 WHOLE PERSON ASSOCIATES, 101 WEST 2ND STREET, SUITE 203, DULUTH MN 55802 • 800-247-6789 • WHOLEPERSON.COM

Qualities of Kindness

The word kindness generally defines a person's ability to be gentle, friendly, and warmhearted toward others. In order to feel kind and friendly, one must either feel very good inside, or act as if one feels good.

Because acts of kindness can reflect a person's complex disposition or inner essence, it helps to ignite the kindness by spending time with people one cares for, spending time in moments that provide one with wonder, and by acting with kindness. All three spiritual connections can help to support a person's ability to be kind and to act with kindness towards others.

Kindness, caring, and empathy all connect to a person's complex dispositions. When someone acts with kindness, one also has the power to nurture one's spiritual side, thus opening oneself up to experiencing more and deeper relationships, and more satisfying moments of wonder and joy.

We can pass along kindness to children only if we feel it ourselves.

On the list below, check off the ways you would describe yourself:

I consider myself to be …

- ☐ benevolent
- ☐ caring
- ☐ compassionate
- ☐ considerate
- ☐ empathetic
- ☐ generous
- ☐ helpful
- ☐ kind
- ☐ ______________________________
- ☐ ______________________________

© 2017 WHOLE PERSON ASSOCIATES, 101 WEST 2ND STREET, SUITE 203, DULUTH MN 55802 • 800-247-6789 • WHOLEPERSON.COM

Benevolence

How would you define benevolence?

Toward whom do you show benevolence?

How do you display your benevolent character to the above people?

How do the above people display benevolence to you?

How can you model benevolence to the children you know?

© 2017 WHOLE PERSON ASSOCIATES, 101 WEST 2ND STREET, SUITE 203, DULUTH MN 55802 • 800-247-6789 • WHOLEPERSON.COM

Caring

How would you define caring?

Toward whom do you show care?

How do you display your caring character to the above people?

How do the above people display that they care about you?

How can you model caring to the children you know?

© 2017 WHOLE PERSON ASSOCIATES, 101 WEST 2ND STREET, SUITE 203, DULUTH MN 55802 • 800-247-6789 • WHOLEPERSON.COM

Compassion

How would you define compassion?

Toward whom do you show compassion?

How do you display your compassionate character to the above people?

How do the above people display compassion to you?

How can you model compassion to the children you know?

© 2017 WHOLE PERSON ASSOCIATES, 101 WEST 2ND STREET, SUITE 203, DULUTH MN 55802 • 800-247-6789 • WHOLEPERSON.COM

Consideration

How would you define consideration?

Toward whom do you show consideration?

How do you display your considerate character to the above people?

How do the above people display consideration to you?

How can you model consideration to the children you know?

© 2017 WHOLE PERSON ASSOCIATES, 101 WEST 2ND STREET, SUITE 203, DULUTH MN 55802 • 800-247-6789 • WHOLEPERSON.COM

Empathy

How would you define empathy?

Toward whom do you show empathy?

How do you display your empathetic character to the above people?

How do the above people display empathy to you?

How can you model empathy to the children you know?

© 2017 WHOLE PERSON ASSOCIATES, 101 WEST 2ND STREET, SUITE 203, DULUTH MN 55802 • 800-247-6789 • WHOLEPERSON.COM

Generosity

How would you define generosity?

Toward whom do you show generosity?

How do you display your generous character to the above people?

How do the above people display generosity to you?

How can you model generosity to the children you know?

Helpfulness

How would you define helpfulness?

Toward whom do you show helpfulness?

How do you display your helpful character to the above people?

How do the above people display helpfulness to you?

How can you model helpfulness to the children you know?

 © 2017 WHOLE PERSON ASSOCIATES, 101 WEST 2ND STREET, SUITE 203, DULUTH MN 55802 • 800-247-6789 • WHOLEPERSON.COM

Kindness

How would you define kindness?

Toward whom do you show kindness?

How do you display your kind character to the above people?

How do the above people display kindness to you?

How can you model kindness to the children you know?

© 2017 WHOLE PERSON ASSOCIATES, 101 WEST 2ND STREET, SUITE 203, DULUTH MN 55802 • 800-247-6789 • WHOLEPERSON.COM

Kindness: Thought-Provoking Quotations

"Kindness is just love with its work boots on." ~ *Author Unknown*

"It's nice to be important, but it's more important to be nice." ~ *Author Unknown*

After reading the above quotations, choose one and write your thoughts, create a poem, or draw a picture to describe your insights.

Quotation ____

© 2017 WHOLE PERSON ASSOCIATES, 101 WEST 2ND STREET, SUITE 203, DULUTH MN 55802 • 800-247-6789 • WHOLEPERSON.COM

Kindness

Ideas, Activities, and Moments for All Caregivers to Share with Children

Kindness emerges from a life filled with strong relationships and time spent in spiritual moments filled with wonder. Therefore, we support children by providing them with love and spiritual moments. We also understand that we don't make children happy when we simply enable them to be receivers of kindness. We escalate their feelings of happiness, improve their well-being, enrich their friendships, and build peace and reduce bullying, by supporting them to be givers as well as receivers of kindness.

- Allow the child to help you clean up and do chores around the house.
- Ask the child for a hug when you need it; offer a hug in return.
- Be kind to people. You will be modeling kindness by example.
- Compliment others with specific details. The child will notice.
- Do not litter. The child will litter if you do.
- Encourage the child to create a card or make something to take to someone who is ill.
- Expect the child to be helpful.
- Give the child appropriate responsibilities in caring for a pet.
- Go with the child to visit people in a skilled care facility, to cheer people up.
- Help a neighbor. Take the child with you.
- Role-model giving to charity.
- Start a ritual. Before birthday or holiday gift-receiving time, with the child, go through the toy chest and select toys to donate to children who could use them.
- Take your child with you when you deliver books or clothing to a donation point.
- Tell children that they have done a good job when they have been helpful. Be specific. Too much empty praise can be harmful. "You did a great job getting all the dog food into the dog bowl."
- Thank the checkout person in the store, who is standing all day, or working on the weekend. When you do it with a child, you are a role model.
- When the child does something kind, use phrases such as:

  "That was kind of you to hold the door open for Mr. Smith,"

  "That was very helpful when you carried Mr. Arnold's groceries." or

  "That was thoughtful of you when you made the get well card for Aunt Betty."
- With the child, bring soup or a meal to someone who is ill.

© 2017 WHOLE PERSON ASSOCIATES, 101 WEST 2ND STREET, SUITE 203, DULUTH MN 55802 • 800-247-6789 • WHOLEPERSON.COM

Notes to Myself

(Thoughts and Ideas)

© 2017 WHOLE PERSON ASSOCIATES, 101 WEST 2ND STREET, SUITE 203, DULUTH MN 55802 • 800-247-6789 • WHOLEPERSON.COM

Things to Do

(Actions to Take)

SECTION 8

Imagination

An Imaginary Friend, Da

At the age of four, my daughter (the third of our four children) had a friend called Da. Da was often with her. We couldn't see Da. But she knew Da was there. When I asked her recently about Da, she said that Da was an old man in a long white robe, and he was her friend.

I also asked her if anyone in our family made fun of her or her relationship with Da, and she said no. Whew! SO glad we respected her imagination!

~ Ester Leutenberg

© 2017 WHOLE PERSON ASSOCIATES, 101 WEST 2ND STREET, SUITE 203, DULUTH MN 55802 • 800-247-6789 • WHOLEPERSON.COM

© 2017 WHOLE PERSON ASSOCIATES, 101 WEST 2ND STREET, SUITE 203, DULUTH MN 55802 • 800-247-6789 • WHOLEPERSON.COM

Imagination

Spirituality is a gift that is always there for everyone. However, just like any gift, it needs to have the bow untied, the ribbon removed, and the box opened. It needs to be taken out of the box. It needs to be acknowledged by the person who is receiving the gift.

Before one can truly acknowledge sparks and sensations as spiritual-ness, one needs to be open to the possibilities of its existence. This requires imagination: the process of forming images or concepts in the mind. These images are most often images of things that are not really visible, just like spirituality. Much of spirituality is unseen, but deeply felt. Children develop imagination through concrete play that eventually turns into representational play. Being playful and having a good sense of humor strengthens one's ability to use imagination and therefore helps one to be open to ideas of leading a spiritual life.

Think about how you used your imagination as a child.

At play *(ex: everyday objects made into a toy.)*

____

____

____

____

____

Imaginary companion *(ex: person, dog, friendly monster, etc.)*

____

____

____

____

____

Body experiences *(ex: sports, exercise, yoga, martial arts, relaxation techniques, solitude.)*

____

____

____

____

____

(Continued on the next page)

© 2017 WHOLE PERSON ASSOCIATES, 101 WEST 2ND STREET, SUITE 203, DULUTH MN 55802 • 800-247-6789 • WHOLEPERSON.COM

Think about how you used your imagination as a child. *(Continued)*

Self-expression *(ex: creating, writing, music, art, dancing.)*

In Relationships *(ex: aware of affection, communication, taking action, being in sync, beliefs.)*

In nature *(ex: animals, unique sights, weather, bodies of water, trees, rocks, or flowers.)*

With yourself *(ex: AHA! moments, illness, wellness, deep breaths, thankfulness, forgiveness, acceptance.)*

© 2017 WHOLE PERSON ASSOCIATES, 101 WEST 2ND STREET, SUITE 203, DULUTH MN 55802 • 800-247-6789 • WHOLEPERSON.COM

Humor: Laughing and Smiling

Laughter has psychological, physiological, social, spiritual, and quality of life benefits. Laughing and smiling are human behaviors.

A baby's first step toward humor is a playful response to actions like bouncing and tickling, body contact that produces laughs, wiggles, and smiles. Infants like interesting sounds. Twelve-hour-old infants will shape their mouth into what looks like a smile at the smell of a banana or other sweet food. True laughter appears a few months later, perhaps when one blows 'raspberries' on the infant's belly.

Memory and imitation help one-year-olds figure out that it is funny to do something unexpected. A one-year-old child may giggle at a game of peek-a-boo or at funny faces. A two-year-old may burst into a fit of giggles upon hearing a fun phrase from a Dr. Seuss book. Placing a sock on a foot is not funny, but placing it on an ear is hysterical to two-year-olds because they realize that it does not belong there. They share that knowledge through laughter. When they place a sock on an ear, they are then making their own jokes.

What are some of your personal experiences as a young child laughing or having a sense of humor?

____

____

____

____

____

A caregiver's encouragement helps children to see the humor in this world, and will help them to see things from many perspectives other than the most obvious. A good sense of humor provides a broad range of important benefits to children, just as it does to adults.

Humor helps children in several ways:

- construct an unreal situation and pretend, much as make-believe play does.
- develop spontaneity.
- enjoy and participate in the playful aspects of life.
- grasp unconventional ideas or ways of thinking.
- handle differences (their own and others') well.
- learn not to take themselves too seriously.
- see beyond the surface of things.

Humor is a catalyst for enhancing a child's imagination and for the child being open to endless possibilities!

A caregiver can support a child's sense of humor by spending some time playing with the child every day. It is important to make a special effort to at least occasionally laugh or otherwise respond to the child's attempts to make you laugh. The more the child's sense of humor is supported at an early age, the more likely the child is to emerge into the teen years and adulthood with a well-developed set of humor skills that support good mental and physical health. It is extremely important for caregivers to be positive role models of humor, remembering that a sense of humor can make life fun.

© 2017 WHOLE PERSON ASSOCIATES, 101 WEST 2ND STREET, SUITE 203, DULUTH MN 55802 • 800-247-6789 • WHOLEPERSON.COM

Adulthood Imagination

In these days, our busy lives, computers, television, automatic toys, etc., often discourage creativity and imagination.

**Today, as an adult,
what kind of play or playfulness sparks your imagination and laughter?**

Childhood Imagination

A child with an active imagination is more alert, flexible, better able to cope, and more likely to grow into a well-balanced, creative, self-assured adult.

What sparks the imagination of a child you know?

© 2017 WHOLE PERSON ASSOCIATES, 101 WEST 2ND STREET, SUITE 203, DULUTH MN 55802 • 800-247-6789 • WHOLEPERSON.COM

Imagination: Thought-Provoking Quotations

"Logic will get you from A to Z; imagination will get you everywhere." ~ *Albert Einstein*

"Imagination does not become great until human beings, given the courage and the strength, use it to create." ~ *Maria Montessori*

After reading the above quotations, choose one and write your thoughts, create a poem, or draw a picture to describe your insights.

Quotation ____

© 2017 WHOLE PERSON ASSOCIATES, 101 WEST 2ND STREET, SUITE 203, DULUTH MN 55802 • 800-247-6789 • WHOLEPERSON.COM

Imagination

Ideas, Activities, and Moments for All Caregivers to Share with Children

Imagination invites our minds to go beyond the concrete to recognize, feel, see, and know what spirituality is and feels like. By opening up ourselves to the possibilities of being spiritual and by using our imaginations to acknowledge this invisible force, we can nurture our own spiritual development. In order to nurture the ability to be imaginative, very young children require a lot of open-ended and unguided time to play. Many children today are often robbed of this treasure of time. To set the stage for play does not require a lot of money, fancy toys, or time with many adults. It does require support, modeling, and a child's ability to see enough of the caregivers in their lives in order to have positive role-models to emulate.

- Allow the child to make choices about what to wear and which toys to play with.
- Ask the child to look at a painting you have at home, or in a gallery or an art museum. Ask the child to ask questions, find details, or make up a story about it.
- Ask "What if . . ." questions about a story, painting, etc.
- Encourage the child to draw, paint, doodle, mold, build, sculpt, etc. Tactile experiences are important, and giving young children free rein over their work is essential!
- Engage in imaginative play with the child. Have a dress up box with old clothes and miscellaneous items. A towel can become a turban. Plastic beads are jewels. Stuffed animals become farm animals.
- Expose the child to diversity.
- Find objects from nature to inspire a child's imagination.
- Gather up string, pieces of sponge, broken pencils, rubber bands, strips of yarn or fabric, wedges of potatoes, etc. Spread some newspaper or a plastic cloth on a table or the floor, put washable paint in small bowls, give the child a large sheet of paper (at least 18 by 24 inches), and see what the child creates.
- Honor a child's imagination.
- Improve your mood and the child's mood by laughing together.
- Judgment has no place when one is being imaginative.
- Laughing together is a way to connect.
- Laughter is contagious! Laugh heartily. The child will laugh with you.
- Leave children alone to use toys as they wish.
- Make up creative stories, rhymes, and songs. Then listen to the child's made up stories, rhymes, and songs.
- Obtain a big box from a refrigerator or large appliance. Or put a tablecloth over a bridge table or dining room table. It can become a house, a cave, a rocket ship, or a time capsule.
- Offer a large blank piece of paper and paints.
- Play with open-ended toys, such as blocks, sand, and water for endless possibilities.
- See pretend as valuable.
- Start a story, ask the child to tell the next sentence, you tell the next, etc.
- Use humor with the child.

© 2017 WHOLE PERSON ASSOCIATES, 101 WEST 2ND STREET, SUITE 203, DULUTH MN 55802 • 800-247-6789 • WHOLEPERSON.COM

Notes to Myself

(Thoughts and Ideas)

© 2017 WHOLE PERSON ASSOCIATES, 101 WEST 2ND STREET, SUITE 203, DULUTH MN 55802 • 800-247-6789 • WHOLEPERSON.COM

Things to Do

(Actions to Take)

SECTION 9

Openness & Acceptance

My Spiritualism Kicked In!

My son died of suicide in 1986, at 30 years of age. The stigma of mental illness was shame, isolation, loneliness, and fear. He asked my husband and me, not to tell anyone that he had a mental illness and we promised him (many times over the eight years he was trying to die by suicide). He ran a business, was a well-known person in the community, and knew people wouldn't treat or feel the same way about him if they learned of his mental illness. In those years, the stigma of mental illness was far worse than it is now. We told no one until the day he died. Then we told everyone. We weren't embarrassed or ashamed. We became advocates for erasing the stigma of mental illness through awareness.

About five years after my son died, I realized that I had broken my promise. I looked up and pensively said, "I hope you're not angry or upset with me. Please give me a sign that it's okay." That night as we drove into our driveway (the same time as we did every day for three years) the sun's rays were like a painting. I pondered … could my son be telling me it is okay? The next night, the exact same thing happened. I then realized that he was 'with me.' At that point, I was open for him to come to us in many other forms and ways. The possibilities were endless. That's when my spiritualism REALLY kicked in.

~ Ester Leutenberg

© 2017 WHOLE PERSON ASSOCIATES, 101 WEST 2ND STREET, SUITE 203, DULUTH MN 55802 • 800-247-6789 • WHOLEPERSON.COM

© 2017 WHOLE PERSON ASSOCIATES, 101 WEST 2ND STREET, SUITE 203, DULUTH MN 55802 • 800-247-6789 • WHOLEPERSON.COM

Openness & Acceptance

Some caregivers welcome the fact that we live in an increasingly diverse and open society. They are open to new people, ideas, and spiritual thoughts. Other caregivers are more hesitant, especially if they haven't had much exposure to people different from themselves with different ideas or spiritual thoughts. As children get older, they are often exposed to cultural differences as their circle of friends, schoolmates, and athletic team members are much more diverse than those of even one generation ago.

Caregivers need to help prepare children to live, learn, and work in communities that will become even more diverse. Modeling tolerance, empathy, and openness to cultures different from their own is important from the very beginning of a child's life. This will lead the child through today and into tomorrow's world.

As a child, which of these ideas, concepts, or cultural aspects, that were different from your own, were you exposed to? Write a few words about your experiences.

- ☐ Behavior ______
- ☐ Beliefs ______
- ☐ Body image ______
- ☐ Clothing ______
- ☐ Emotional/mental issues ______
- ☐ Ethnicity ______
- ☐ Family ______
- ☐ Financial status ______
- ☐ Foods ______
- ☐ Learning disabilities ______
- ☐ LGBTQ+ ______
- ☐ Neighborhood diversity ______
- ☐ Physical disabilities ______
- ☐ Race ______
- ☐ Religion ______
- ☐ Social status ______
- ☐ Spirituality ______
- ☐ Values ______
- ☐ Other ______
- ☐ Other ______
- ☐ Other ______
- ☐ Other ______

© 2017 WHOLE PERSON ASSOCIATES, 101 WEST 2ND STREET, SUITE 203, DULUTH MN 55802 • 800-247-6789 • WHOLEPERSON.COM

One's Openness & Acceptance Can Change

Which of the items that you checked on the previous page eventually changed from your childhood to adulthood?

When and under what circumstance did it affect you?

In what ways did you become more or less open? Explain.

In what ways did you become more or less accepting? Explain.

© 2017 WHOLE PERSON ASSOCIATES, 101 WEST 2ND STREET, SUITE 203, DULUTH MN 55802 • 800-247-6789 • WHOLEPERSON.COM

Openness & Acceptance with Children

How do you display openness and acceptance to the children you know?

How do the children you know display openness and acceptance?

© 2017 WHOLE PERSON ASSOCIATES, 101 WEST 2ND STREET, SUITE 203, DULUTH MN 55802 • 800-247-6789 • WHOLEPERSON.COM

Opening Up to a Spiritual Life

Identify some of your experiences that can't be explained or dismissed.

If you've had subtle feelings with vague meanings that bring questions to you, list them.

Describe experiences you have had, that were above or beyond the realm of normal.

In what ways were these moments spiritual for you?

© 2017 WHOLE PERSON ASSOCIATES, 101 WEST 2ND STREET, SUITE 203, DULUTH MN 55802 • 800-247-6789 • WHOLEPERSON.COM

Openness & Acceptance: Thought-Provoking Quotations

"Our entire life consists ultimately in accepting ourselves as we are." ~ *Jean Anouilh*

"Let go of certainty. The opposite isn't uncertainty. It's openness, curiosity and a willingness to embrace paradox, rather than choose up sides. The ultimate challenge is to accept ourselves exactly as we are, but never stop trying to learn and grow." ~ *Tony Schwartz*

After reading the above quotations, choose one and write your thoughts, create a poem, or draw a picture to describe your insights.

Quotation ____

© 2017 WHOLE PERSON ASSOCIATES, 101 WEST 2ND STREET, SUITE 203, DULUTH MN 55802 • 800-247-6789 • WHOLEPERSON.COM

Openness & Acceptance

Ideas, Activities, and Moments for All Caregivers to Share with Children

Openness and acceptance invite one to sense the possibility of spirituality. The existence of these deeply felt feelings help to peacefully guide us through life. These feelings invite the mind to go beyond the concrete - to recognize, feel, see, and be aware of spirituality and what it feels like. By opening up ourselves to the possibility of being spiritual and by using our imaginations to acknowledge this invisible force, we can nurture our own spiritual development. In order to nurture an ability to be open, very young children require open-ended and unguided time to play. Creating an atmosphere in which differences are accepted and appreciated is imperative. To set the stage for play does not require many toys or a lot of money. To set the stage for openness and acceptance requires support, role-modeling, and encouraging a child's awareness and appreciation of differences.

- Arrange play with children from a variety of cultures and diverse physical attributes.
- Be open and accepting with the child and the child will be the same with others.
- Do not get involved in disputes between children unless absolutely necessary as children can and will often work things out.
- Encourage the child to draw, paint, doodle, mold, build, sculpt, etc. Tactile experiences are important, and giving young children free rein over their work is the key to young children showing their passions and preferences!
- Expose the child to diversity.
- Give the child the opportunity to play as long as the child wishes, making personal choices and changes.
- Judgment has no place when one is being open.
- Make up creative stories, rhymes, and songs, and listen to the child's stories, rhymes, and songs.
- Model openness by being accepting to all people of all diversities.
- Obtain a big box from a refrigerator or large appliance. Or put a tablecloth over a table. It can become a house, a cave, a rocket ship, or a time capsule.
- Offer open-ended and unguided time to play.
- Promote openness to come into play.
- See pretending as valuable.
- Take a paper bag and go for a walk. Invite the child to pick up attractive or unusual nature objects. Later, ask the child to sort the objects, or make up a story with the objects.
- Toddlers love colorful picture books. Read repeatedly, pointing and saying the words. Talk about the pictures.

© 2017 WHOLE PERSON ASSOCIATES, 101 WEST 2ND STREET, SUITE 203, DULUTH MN 55802 • 800-247-6789 • WHOLEPERSON.COM

© 2017 WHOLE PERSON ASSOCIATES, 101 WEST 2ND STREET, SUITE 203, DULUTH MN 55802 • 800-247-6789 • WHOLEPERSON.COM

Notes to Myself

(Thoughts and Ideas)

© 2017 WHOLE PERSON ASSOCIATES, 101 WEST 2ND STREET, SUITE 203, DULUTH MN 55802 • 800-247-6789 • WHOLEPERSON.COM

Things to Do

(Actions to Take)

SECTION 10

Gratitude

Grateful All Around

When Aunt Lori came to visit she brought the children, ages eight, six, and three, beautiful new lunch bags for the beginning of school. One was blue, one brown, and one yellow. She asked the children who knew which was for which child. One child reached for the brown one. The other two wanted the blue lunch bag leaving the yellow one unclaimed. Without any encouragement, the oldest child offered to relinquish his bag so that each child might feel contentment, each holding a bag that was satisfying.

Since these were gifts, it was Aunt Lori who first modeled gratitude for the selfless act that made her gifts very much appreciated by all three children. In this way, everyone left the scene feeling gratitude.

Aunt Lori was grateful that the children appreciated her gifts. The eight-year-old was grateful he had done something benevolent. The younger two children were simply grateful for their gifts. None of this went unnoticed by their grandmother who watched the entire scenario unfold. She was grateful for the entire moment. The atmosphere around this small group of family members was peaceful and joyful instead of filled with whines and cries, something everyone was also grateful for having avoided.

~ Deborah Schein

© 2017 WHOLE PERSON ASSOCIATES, 101 WEST 2ND STREET, SUITE 203, DULUTH MN 55802 • 800-247-6789 • WHOLEPERSON.COM

Gratitude

Gratitude is both an emotion and an attitude that emerges when one experiences positive moments, and one is thankful and happy about these moments. Experiencing a spiritual moment can produce feelings of gratitude whether these feelings emerge from relationships, moments of wonder, or acts of kindness. Simply stated, gratitude is showing appreciation and thankfulness for what one has, what one experiences, and how one feels.

In order to model gratitude for a child, one must first feel grateful, and then show gratitude by expressing it daily. Gratitude can be expressed through words, prayers, blessings, art, journal writing, gifts, hugs, kisses, etc.

Feelings of gratitude put one in touch with one's spiritual development or one's spiritual self.

For whom and what are you grateful?

Your list can be small things, every day things, or large things.

____

____

____

____

____

____

____

____

How do you express your gratitude?

____

____

____

____

____

____

____

____

© 2017 WHOLE PERSON ASSOCIATES, 101 WEST 2ND STREET, SUITE 203, DULUTH MN 55802 • 800-247-6789 • WHOLEPERSON.COM

Role-Modeling Gratitude

How do you show your gratitude in the presence of children you know?

What kind of gratitude do you see children display and how do you support it?

© 2017 WHOLE PERSON ASSOCIATES, 101 WEST 2ND STREET, SUITE 203, DULUTH MN 55802 • 800-247-6789 • WHOLEPERSON.COM

Gratitude: Thought-Provoking Quotations

"Gratitude unlocks the fullness of life. It turns what we have into enough, and more. It turns denial into acceptance, chaos to order, confusion to clarity. It can turn a meal into a feast, a house into a home, a stranger into a friend." ~ *Melody Beattie*

"Accept the children the way we accept trees – with gratitude because they are a blessing – but do not have expectations or desires. You don't expect trees to change, you love them as they are." ~ *Isabel Allende*

After reading the above quotations, choose one and write your thoughts, create a poem, or draw a picture to describe your insights.

Quotation ____

© 2017 WHOLE PERSON ASSOCIATES, 101 WEST 2ND STREET, SUITE 203, DULUTH MN 55802 • 800-247-6789 • WHOLEPERSON.COM

Gratitude

Ideas, Activities, and Moments for All Caregivers to Share with Children

Gratitude is a complex emotion that one feels. Each person has an inner ability to feel grateful, whether the person has been blessed with abundance or whether the person has been deprived and is grateful for every little thing. Whatever the reason, gratitude is an emotion one feels and then can express. Expressions of one's gratitude have a strong relationship to feeling satisfaction in living and life. Some people may use prayers and blessings. Others might use hugs, gifts, or cards to express their gratitude. Whatever the source of feeling gratitude and method of expressing it, gratitude helps one to feel one's own spirituality.

- Appreciate the beauty found in nature with the child.
- Assist the child in writing a "Gratitude Letter" to someone who enhances the child's life.
- Be respectful and grateful for differences.
- Buy a pair of oversized or fun-looking glasses and call them the "Gratitude Glasses." Use these as a prop to focus the child's attention on the things for which the child is grateful.
- Collect loose change together for a time period and then donate it to an organization the family agrees on together.
- Decorate a "Gratitude Box" so the child can record grateful thoughts and store them in the box. Review these comments regularly and make sure to provide your own contributions too!
- Develop and grow many relationships and support the child to do the same. Strong relationships help to create feelings of gratitude.
- Give the child your time. Be mindful.
- Help the child to appreciate the blessings in the world.
- Make up small blessings with a child to express gratitude for any situation – seeing a new baby, having a tooth fall out, learning how to tie one's shoes, etc.
- Name your blessings and then ask the child to do the same. Include being grateful for the child.
- Point out the wonderment in all kinds of weather with the child.
- Read books that convey the value of gratitude to the child.
- Role-model expressing gratitude through words, writing, small gifts, or acts of kindness.
- Set examples by always saying Thank you, You're welcome, I appreciate that.
- Start a gratitude journal with the child or a group of children.
- Stop while on a walk to show gratitude to the earth.
- Support the child's accomplishments, and encourage the child to thank those who've helped.
- Tell the child what you are grateful for today and ask, What are you grateful for today?

© 2017 WHOLE PERSON ASSOCIATES, 101 WEST 2ND STREET, SUITE 203, DULUTH MN 55802 • 800-247-6789 • WHOLEPERSON.COM

Notes to Myself

(Thoughts and Ideas)

© 2017 WHOLE PERSON ASSOCIATES, 101 WEST 2ND STREET, SUITE 203, DULUTH MN 55802 • 800-247-6789 • WHOLEPERSON.COM

Things to Do

(Actions to Take)

© 2017 WHOLE PERSON ASSOCIATES, 101 WEST 2ND STREET, SUITE 203, DULUTH MN 55802 • 800-247-6789 • WHOLEPERSON.COM

Section 11

Breath and Presence

Being Present

Recently I went for a walk in a local park. I happened upon an older woman leaning over a bridge. I looked to see where she was looking. From the bridge, my eyes saw only water. Then I suddenly saw at least twenty ducks or more sitting on concrete steps leading down to the stream. Then the woman said to me, "Look, can you see the turtles?" "Turtles," I thought. "Where? I don't see any turtles."

Then there they were - as clear to me as the water. One was swimming under the bridge. My young cousins, ages seven and twelve, their father, my husband, and several other people on the bridge all hurried to the other side of the bridge to see the turtles emerge.

By this time my eyes had adjusted to this spiritual moment. I could now see not only the one turtle, but many turtles swimming in the water.

~ Deborah Schein

© 2017 WHOLE PERSON ASSOCIATES, 101 WEST 2ND STREET, SUITE 203, DULUTH MN 55802 • 800-247-6789 • WHOLEPERSON.COM

© 2017 WHOLE PERSON ASSOCIATES, 101 WEST 2ND STREET, SUITE 203, DULUTH MN 55802 • 800-247-6789 • WHOLEPERSON.COM

Feeling Breath and Acknowledging Presence

When one develops a growing sense of self-awareness and an ability to be mindful, then one also begins to feel inner breath and outer presence. This section is about feeling one's own breath and acknowledging one's own presence which ultimately supports one's ability to develop deep connections needed for nurturing spiritual development.

Breath

When one takes time to breathe with mindfulness, that breath can be felt as it travels through the body nurturing one's organs and muscles, including the brain. With help from the brain and nervous system, it is possible to feel and hear each breath as it enters through the nose or mouth. As one inhales, or breathes in, the belly should expand; as one exhales, the belly contracts. In this way, the entire body is touched by each breath that one takes. Simultaneously, one's senses, through skin, eyes, ears, touch, taste, and smell become heightened thus helping to create the deep connection within oneself that nurtures one's inner sense of spirituality. The word breath is often associated with breath of life which is sometimes given as another definition of spirituality.

Natural Breathing

Many breathing exercises focus on abdominal or diaphragmatic breathing. This means breathing in a way that makes the stomach expand and contract. This is known as a natural way of breathing – the kind of breathing done by babies. This type of breathing is very effective. It can also help one connect to that inner self known as one's essence or spirit and can begin to unwrap this lovely gift found within.

If you can, watch a baby breathe. This will give you an idea of what it means to breathe naturally. Notice that babies breathe in slow, deep, rhythmic patterns. The belly expands with each slow breath and contracts when each breath is released. You can do this too.

- Find a quiet comfortable place to sit.
- Close your eyes.
- Consciously breathe slowly through your nose.
- Some people like to count during this time. If you choose to count you might begin with four slow breaths in and four slow breaths out. Add on slowly as you continue deep breathing.
- Attempt to make your breathing gentle and smooth, slow, and effortless. One inhale should lead quietly into an exhale. Make each moment last as long as you can without holding your breath.

© 2017 WHOLE PERSON ASSOCIATES, 101 WEST 2ND STREET, SUITE 203, DULUTH MN 55802 • 800-247-6789 • WHOLEPERSON.COM

Breath and Meditation

The Dalai Lama's Summary of the Practice of Breath and Meditation

Set aside some time early in the morning when your mind is freshest and clearest. Begin by setting aside ten or fifteen minutes, and reserve for yourself a couple of five-minute interludes later in the day. Find a comfortable position and begin by focusing on your breathing. A few minutes a day can help you overcome any tendency toward excessive worrying, useless obsessions, or anxiety over having more to do than you have time for. It may be helpful to focus on a flower, or a painting, or some object of religious devotion, "or you may imagine looking down from a mountaintop where you have an unimpeded view in every direction." You might want to focus on compassion, patience, tolerance, or forgiveness.

The Dalai Lama's own words offer the best summary:

"In a typical session, we begin by settling our mind through breathing. We then choose our object of meditation and focus our attention on it. When we notice our mind wandering, we gently bring it back to our object of meditation. When we wish to end our session, we can do some deep breathing exercises once again so that we finish in a relaxed state of mind."

How does your mind and body react when you focus on your breath and breathing?

____

____

____

When do you, or could you, use deep breathing exercises?

____

____

____

If you have meditated, what were your experiences?

____

____

____

You might want to try the Dalai Lama's recommendations above and/or the natural breathing exercise on the previous page.

© 2017 WHOLE PERSON ASSOCIATES, 101 WEST 2ND STREET, SUITE 203, DULUTH MN 55802 • 800-247-6789 • WHOLEPERSON.COM

Presence

Presence makes each of us visible to ourselves and to others. It is a way of saying, "Here I am." Presence is needed in order to form relationships and deep connections. Being present brings one into relationships with other persons, places, or things.

In such moments all of one's senses are awakened so that one can really see and hear each other, and one can see another's inner being, like in the movie Avatar in which the characters could see beyond external images into each other's inner soul, and they could hear beyond the spoken word. In such a state of presence, all of one's senses are awakened to support one's connections.

This kind of presence can be defined as spiritual-ness, which implies becoming or being full of spirit, full of wonderment, awe, and connectedness with the world. The sparks that emanate from such moments can nurture one's own spiritual development, as well as the spirituality of others.

The Importance of Being Present

Presence helps individuals reflect and connect more deeply and with greater meaning. This means that these moments can become powerful sources for spiritual growth and development.

Being present also helps each of us look deeper within ourselves and into those we know in order to observe the power of each individual's uniqueness, personality, character, or dispositions. With this knowledge, we can better understand what makes each of us tick. Only then can we truly nurture ourselves and others by providing for and supporting spiritual moments as each of us is touched by different people, places, and things.

Other attributes such as awe also play into building one's ability to be present. Experiencing awe can help individuals develop feelings of gratitude and purpose. Ultimately, feelings of gratitude and purpose help people make more ethical decisions, and being ethical is another way of saying that people act in pro-social ways. Ultimately, becoming pro-social is required for building an inner spiritual system.

Being present also means being responsive and responsible in all relationships. When one is more responsive and responsible, one is more likely to model presence for the children in one's care. One interpretation of this is to model being welcoming, caring, and open. Many adults say that they are welcoming, caring, and open, but often fail to reflect upon their actions and often do not live up to their own vision of themselves, or how they model these for children.

© 2017 WHOLE PERSON ASSOCIATES, 101 WEST 2ND STREET, SUITE 203, DULUTH MN 55802 • 800-247-6789 • WHOLEPERSON.COM

Being Present

In your life, what does *being present* mean to you?

How can you bring or increase moments of presence into your life?

At this time, how does your ability to be present affect your relationships with children?

In the future, how can your ability to be present affect your relationships with children?

© 2017 WHOLE PERSON ASSOCIATES, 101 WEST 2ND STREET, SUITE 203, DULUTH MN 55802 • 800-247-6789 • WHOLEPERSON.COM

Supporting Children's Ability to Be Present

When we as adults can be in touch with our own ability to be present, we can better support spiritual moments with children. It is important to acknowledge that young children live in a present here-and-now state of being. Many people, places, and things are new to them. There are many times and many ways in which they find themselves filled with wonderment, awe, joy, and inner peace. If you watch children closely, you may see sparks of spiritual-ness in their eyes and body posture, as well as in their ability to focus or exude calm, not frenetic excitement in what they are doing.

To support young children's ability to be present, they need …

- caregivers to provide guidance.
- caregivers to support and share in their choices.
- time every day to play without being told what to do or how to do it.
- to be in nature, surrounded by light, color, and beauty.
- to be recognized as individuals who have distinct likes and dislikes.
- to make their own choices about how to spend their time.
- to spend many of their waking hours with people who care about them.

Following these suggestions can help the caregivers support the spiritual growth and development of young children by helping them become more present.

Nurturing children's spiritual development in these ways will also support all other developmental domains: cognitive, social, emotional, and physical development.

How do you support children's ability to be present?

____

____

____

____

What more can you do to support children's ability to be present?

____

____

____

____

© 2017 WHOLE PERSON ASSOCIATES, 101 WEST 2ND STREET, SUITE 203, DULUTH MN 55802 • 800-247-6789 • WHOLEPERSON.COM

Supporting a Child's Spirituality

What do you do to support a child's spirituality?

What other thoughts do you have about spiritual development?

What other small or big questions do you have about spiritual development?

How can you continue the dialogue about spirituality or spiritual development?

(Example: Study or support group)

If you wish to share thoughts with us, feel free to contact us at:

ester36@gmail.com

© 2017 WHOLE PERSON ASSOCIATES, 101 WEST 2ND STREET, SUITE 203, DULUTH MN 55802 • 800-247-6789 • WHOLEPERSON.COM

Breath and Presence: Thought-Provoking Quotations

"Feelings come and go like clouds on a windy day. Conscious breathing is my anchor." ~ *Thich Nhat Hanh*

"Do not dwell in the past, do not dream of the future, concentrate the mind on the present moment." ~ *Buddha*

After reading the above quotations, choose one and write your thoughts, create a poem, or draw a picture to describe your insights.

Quotation ____

© 2017 WHOLE PERSON ASSOCIATES, 101 WEST 2ND STREET, SUITE 203, DULUTH MN 55802 • 800-247-6789 • WHOLEPERSON.COM

Breath and Presence

Ideas, Activities, and Moments for All Caregivers to Share with Children

Sometimes spirit is referred to as breath or the small voice within that is one's internal "self."
In this way, being mindful of one's breath helps one to become more aware of one's inner self. When one develops a growing sense of self-awareness and an ability to be mindful, one also begins to feel inner breath and outer presence.

Presence makes each person more visible to self and to others. It is a way of saying, "Here I am." Presence is needed in order to form relationships and deep connections. Being present brings one into relationships with others. For children all relationships are important, even relationships with inanimate objects.

- Allow yourself to breathe slowly together with the child; watch how your bodies move in and out with each breath.
- Ask the child to share with you how it feels to take a deep breath or to breathe slowly.
- Breathe onto a mirror with the child.
- Breathe outdoors on a cold day and watch the 'steam' come out.
- Encourage the child to stay focused on what is happening now. Look at what the child is focusing on.
- Establish your own breath and presence practices to be able to role-model for the child.
- Give time for a child to be alone and present, to play without being told what to do.
- Help a child to follow their breath as it moves throughout the body to the head, toes, and fingers.
- Invite children to explore their bodies for places in which air escapes (nose, mouth).
- Listen to your breathing and to the child's breathing; listen to each other as you both breathe in unison.
- Notice how the simple act of taking a deep breath can change how you feel. Try it. Encourage your child to try it with you.
- Practice meditation with the child.
- Put a stuffed animal on the child's belly when the child is lying down. Tell the child to watch it going up and down.
- Request that the child describe what is seen, heard, smelled, and touched during a walk on the beach, in the woods, etc.
- Spend some alone time in the morning before interacting with the child to allow yourself time to be present. The child will benefit.
- Walk in a park with the child and take a few minutes to just look around. Stop and breathe together. You are both present in that moment.

© 2017 WHOLE PERSON ASSOCIATES, 101 WEST 2ND STREET, SUITE 203, DULUTH MN 55802 • 800-247-6789 • WHOLEPERSON.COM

Notes to Myself

(Thoughts and Ideas)

© 2017 WHOLE PERSON ASSOCIATES, 101 WEST 2ND STREET, SUITE 203, DULUTH MN 55802 • 800-247-6789 • WHOLEPERSON.COM

Things to Do

(Actions to Take)

SECTION 12

The BIG Picture: The System of Spiritual Development

Dancing Rainbows

I taught in a school where the four-year-olds decided they wanted to make a chandelier. Their teacher purchased many small glass prisms and the children tied the prisms together in such a way that it did in fact look like a chandelier. Then they searched the classroom for the right place to hang it. They chose a large sunny window. Once it was hung, every sunny day from 10:10 to 10:25 the rainbow would come and dance upon the walls, the floors, and even upon the children themselves. This amazing child-made chandelier provided the children and their families many opportunities to experience and discuss the interconnection of the earth and its elements with us the people who live upon it.

The children began to ask questions: "When will the sun come again?" "Why does the sun shine?" "Where does it go when it is not shining?" "What happens to the rainbow when it leaves our classroom?" "Why is it cloudy today?" "Who makes the clouds?" Big questions such as these eventually lead young children and their families to contemplate both their relationship with the earth and the possibility of transcendence defined as existence or experience beyond the normal or physical level.

It is amazing to contemplate that by placing some prisms in our classroom window we were all - children and adults alike - transported to a deep level of inquiry.

~ Deborah Schein

© 2017 WHOLE PERSON ASSOCIATES, 101 WEST 2ND STREET, SUITE 203, DULUTH MN 55802 • 800-247-6789 • WHOLEPERSON.COM

© 2017 WHOLE PERSON ASSOCIATES, 101 WEST 2ND STREET, SUITE 203, DULUTH MN 55802 • 800-247-6789 • WHOLEPERSON.COM

Spiritual Development

The goal of this book, *Nurturing Spiritual Development in Children by Understanding Our Own Spirituality,* is to present caregivers a definition of spiritual development that can be used for all children. Each human being is born with some ability to make connections, build relationships, feel wonder, and act kindly. It is therefore the responsibility of each caregiver to insure that spiritual development is acknowledged, nurtured, and honored. The various components of spiritual development shared with you within this book offer a system that begins with stages that then blossom into a thriving system capable of supporting itself.

Spiritual development can be further expanded as one becomes more aware of its power and more open to the ability to engage in spiritual moments.

How would you define your spiritual development?

What are your plans in relationship to your own spirituality?

What are your plans in relationship to the spirituality of the children you know?

© 2017 WHOLE PERSON ASSOCIATES, 101 WEST 2ND STREET, SUITE 203, DULUTH MN 55802 • 800-247-6789 • WHOLEPERSON.COM

In The Beginning

The following diagram illustrates the very beginning of the **system of spiritual development**. It is a way of looking at spirituality as it emerges at the **beginning, at birth**. Initially, spiritual development begins with love. It is love that ignites a child's ability to make connections, form relationships, and develop self-awareness. The first arrow connects these qualities to a child's need to experience spiritual moments of wonderment, awe, joy, and inner peace in ways that speak to each child's unique basic dispositions. The flow of spiritual development continues as children innately learn to respond to the external world through acts of care, kindness, empathy, and reverence. These acts help to strengthen one's complex dispositions. When these qualities are in place, a system of spiritual development exists. This system can be completed very early in life as well as strengthened later.

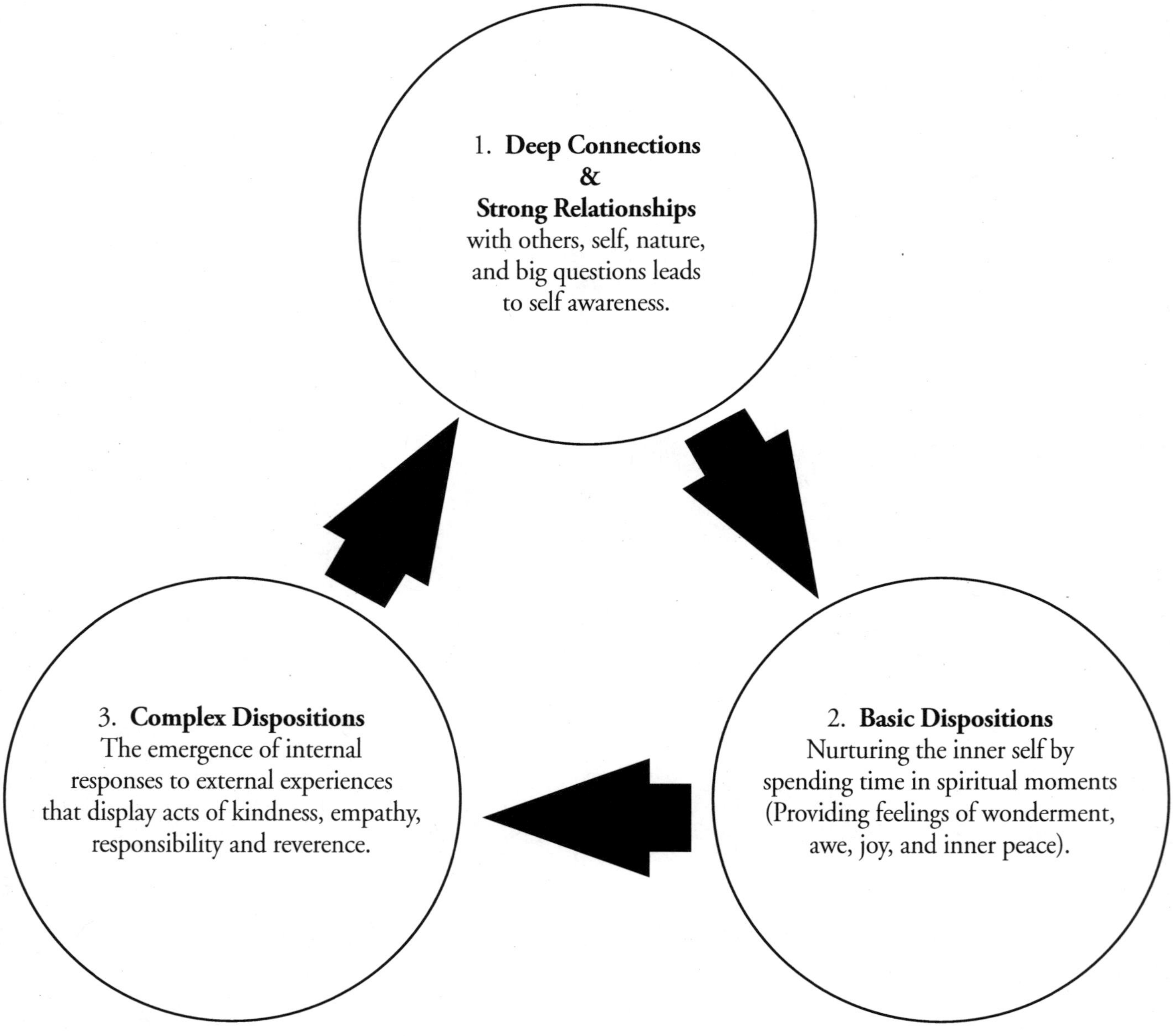

© 2017 WHOLE PERSON ASSOCIATES, 101 WEST 2ND STREET, SUITE 203, DULUTH MN 55802 • 800-247-6789 • WHOLEPERSON.COM

The System of Spiritual Development in ACTION!

The system of spiritual development is now complete. With this completion, other qualities of spirituality have emerged as reflected throughout the pages of this book. Spiritual moments, caregiver love, mindfulness and mindsight, imagination, openness and acceptance, gratitude, and breath and presence are also important ingredients needed to nurture and sustain this system of spiritual development.

We also believe that for young children and adults who are fortunate to have developed a working internal system of spirituality, the next steps focus upon one's ability to understand and take in the values and moral responsibilities of the society or culture in which one lives. It is our hope that such steps lead individuals to strive for a more peaceful world for themselves, family, community, and the world.

MOVING FORWARD

The good news is that in order to move forward, all of the parts of this system are available to everyone almost all of the time. The system begins with love and deep connections. This is the part of the system that holds the need for love in people's lives and opportunities to experience deep connections in spiritual moments. It is in everyone's power to seek the love and connectedness needed to nurture one's own spiritual development. If one is not receiving love, one can learn to offer love to others, which almost always results in love being returned. Through love, spiritual development is strengthened, and it is also distinctively felt internally. Experiencing these internal feelings help people to better know who they are. In this way, a sense of self develops. This is true at any age.

Another part of the system of spiritual development is in knowing oneself so well that one knows what makes oneself tick. This is about knowing one's dispositions and then filling the dispositions (or personal likes) through moments that provide one with wonderment, awe, joy, and inner peace. This can happen during a walk in nature while taking time to breathe, feeling present or mindful, using one's imagination and showing gratitude. All can be done almost any time of the day.

What makes YOU tick?

____

____

____

____

____

____

© 2017 WHOLE PERSON ASSOCIATES, 101 WEST 2ND STREET, SUITE 203, DULUTH MN 55802 • 800-247-6789 • WHOLEPERSON.COM

Nurturing Spirituality Any Time and Any Place

Close your eyes right now and think of a beautiful space that helps you feel amazing. You are filling your system of spiritual development with a moment of wonder and it does not even cost a penny!

Describe the beautiful space that you saw just now.

The final part of the system of spiritual development has to do with how one presents oneself to the outside world. Once one feels those moments of wonderment, awe, joy, and inner peace, one is more apt to act with care, kindness, empathy, and inner peace, thus helping one to become a better citizen of the world.

How do you present yourself to the outside world?

© 2017 WHOLE PERSON ASSOCIATES, 101 WEST 2ND STREET, SUITE 203, DULUTH MN 55802 • 800-247-6789 • WHOLEPERSON.COM

The Big Picture: Thought-Provoking Quotations

"Spirituality is not adopting more beliefs and assumptions but uncovering the best in you." ~ *Amit Ray*

"We live surrounded by an increasingly complex matrix of impulses allowing strangers of all sorts (TV, media, Internet) to interfere in our children's mental, emotional and spiritual development. Understanding this intricate network, and how the human brain interacts with it, is increasingly becoming our door to happiness and health." ~ *Natasa Pantovic Nuit*

After reading the above quotations, choose one and write your thoughts, create a poem, or draw a picture to describe your insights.

Quotation ____

© 2017 WHOLE PERSON ASSOCIATES, 101 WEST 2ND STREET, SUITE 203, DULUTH MN 55802 • 800-247-6789 • WHOLEPERSON.COM

It's Your Choice!

Because spiritual development is defined as a system, it can be nurtured through any of these avenues at any time. Each part actually strengthens the whole of the system. One act of kindness can help you feel more loving and lovable. One act of love can open you up to feeling more moments of wonderment. All the parts are interconnected.

The trick is in knowing that this system of spiritual development exists and is there for you throughout your life, and for the children you care for and love. It is our belief that in nurturing one's spiritual development, one can choose to create a life that will benefit both self and society, because the final result of this system is the creation of people who desire and will to sustain a spiritual life with hope for a peace-filled future.

You Choose

You choose
You choose
You choose
You choose to love and be loved
You choose to connect with others
You choose to develop a sense of self for both you and the world to see.

You choose
You choose
You choose
You choose to breathe deeply
You choose to be content
You choose to feel joy and wonderment that reflects your inner "me."

You choose
You choose
You choose
You choose to act kindly
You choose to act with care
You choose these actions in order to become the spiritual person you strive to be.

You choose
You choose
You choose

~ Deborah Schein

© 2017 WHOLE PERSON ASSOCIATES, 101 WEST 2ND STREET, SUITE 203, DULUTH MN 55802 • 800-247-6789 • WHOLEPERSON.COM

Notes to Myself

(Thoughts and Ideas)

© 2017 WHOLE PERSON ASSOCIATES, 101 WEST 2ND STREET, SUITE 203, DULUTH MN 55802 • 800-247-6789 • WHOLEPERSON.COM

Things to Do

(Actions to Take)

© 2017 WHOLE PERSON ASSOCIATES, 101 WEST 2ND STREET, SUITE 203, DULUTH MN 55802 • 800-247-6789 • WHOLEPERSON.COM

ABOUT THE AUTHORS

Ester R.A. Leutenberg has worked in the mental health field for many years as a publisher, author, and advocate for those suffering from loss. She personally experienced a devastating loss when her son Mitchell, after struggling with a mental illness for eight years, died by suicide in 1986.

Soon after Mitchell's death, as a way of both healing and helping others, Ester co-founded Wellness Reproductions & Publishing with her daughter Kathy Khalsa and they developed these therapeutic products: The *SEALS* series for teen-agers, the *Life Management Skills* series for adults, and a variety of other therapeutic card, board, and bingo games, balloons, and posters.

Ester has co-written the following series of reproducible activity workbooks and card decks created for facilitators: *GriefWork, Mental Health & Life Skills, Teen Mental Health & Life Skills, Mind-Body Wellness, Coping, Transitional Life Skills for Teens, Erasing the Stigma of Mental Health through Awareness, and Working with Families.* Some of the individual books she has co-written include *Creating a Healthy Balanced Life, Motivation, The Complete Caregiver Guide, Veterans Surviving and Thriving, Breaking Up is Hard to Do, and Life Skills to Help Teens Balance WAY TOO MUCH!*

Deborah L. Schein, PhD has been an early childhood educator since 1972. She received a bachelor's degree in psychology, a master's degree in education with a focus on curriculum and instruction. She spent many years teaching in early childhood classrooms in urban and suburban settings, and at numerous colleges. More recently, she completed a Ph.D in early childhood education, researching a definition of spiritual development for young children. This quest began when a young child came to her excitedly holding a worm in his hand. At this moment Deb realized that a language of spiritual development did not exist in this inner city school and possibly from most early childhood programs.

Deborah currently works as an educational consultant and teaches early childhood graduate courses online. She also offers workshops across the country for national movements and participates in webinars about the connection between spiritual development and nature education for young children.

Deborah has co-authored two books, *What's Jewish about Butterflies,* and *The Great Outdoors,* She is currently writing a book that introduces a definition of spiritual development to early childhood educators. It is Deb's goal to help others nurture the spiritual life of children.

ABOUT THE ILLUSTRATOR

Amy Leutenberg Brodsky, LISW-S works assisting children and adults in psychiatric crisis. Amy combines her skills and talents as a social worker and artist, and is well known for her creative illustrations of the Emotions product line, therapeutic games, and over 80 books with Wellness Reproductions and Publishing and with Whole Person Associates … and now, *Nurturing Spiritual Development in Children by Understanding Our Own Spirituality.*

WholePerson

Whole Person Associates is the leading publisher of training resources for professionals who empower people to create and maintain healthy lifestyles. Our creative resources will help you work effectively with your clients in the areas of stress management, wellness promotion, mental health, and life skills.

Please visit us at our web site: **WholePerson.com**.
You can check out our entire line of products, place an order, request our print catalog, and sign up for our monthly special notifications.

Whole Person Associates
800-247-6789
Books@WholePerson.com